Pillars of Mt. Zion:

History of the Branom Community in Western
Hopkins County

Billy D. Haddock

Copyright © 2018 by Silent Partners , College Station, Texas

ISBN-13: 978-0-9669608-4-6

DEDICATION

First, this work is dedicated to remembering: to remember the sacrifices made for our freedom, and even more so to remember that the men, women, and children all involved in & affected by life since the beginning, were not just statistics: they were people just like we are, with the same hopes, dreams, and fears.

Second, this work is dedicated to the power of love: "that the power of LOVE is more important than the love of things, money, religion or power, and when people realize that the most important things in this life are NOT things, the world will finally know peace."

Third, this work is dedicated to the descendants who follow: for any ancestor who wants to have a historical perspective of their family, where they came from, risks they took and which ultimately gives one a broader perspective of how they fit in the grand scheme.

- Billy D. Haddock, Spring 2018

ACKNOWLEDGMENTS

We have a debt of gratitude to the people, both deceased and living, who gathered information that serve as primary sources for details included in this book: Mrs. June Tuck, of the Hopkins County Historical Society, for example.

We are deeply indebted to Jesse Leona BUTLER Broadfoot, for her work in gathering the facts and publishing the booklet entitled, *History Highlights of the Mt Zion Churches and Cemetery*. This source was published in 1967 before the Mt Zion Cemetery Association was formed. This little jewel is a primary, beginning source for the information in this book.

Next, is Yvonne Stewart Rollins and her 2002 publication entitled, *Mt. Zion: its history, its churches, its schools, its families, and its folks*. Other sources of importance are the works of McCuistion (McCuistion 1995) and his history of Lamar County, T.C. Richardson and his work on the history of East Texas, particularly Hopkins County. Finally, my sister, Maredia Haddock Cunningham, helping me remember specific families.

Many of the sources of information were taken from the internet, which was in the public domain. Gloria Mayfield and her work with the Cemeteries of Texas are acknowledged as a useful internet source. Ancestry.com was a major contributor and was not specifically cited, but widely used as a source of details about individuals named herein.

"Home is where one starts from. As we grow older the world becomes stranger, the pattern more complicated of dead and living. Not the intense moment, isolated, with no before and after, but a lifetime burning in every moment. And not the lifetime of one man only, but of old stones that cannot be deciphered." ----- T. S. Eliot, 1888-1965, "Four Quartets, East Coker" (1940)

Preface

Communities are a web of interactions among the environment, the economy and society. There are many ways to measure the growth and quality of life of a Community[1]. I have reached for the common methods: land ownership, churches, cemeteries, cities, government, lodges, methods of transportation, merchants, service (including government and medical), etc. Recent research cites contemporary issues such as:

- Community Safety – using the indexed crime rate

- Safety in the Home – using family violence incidents

- Adult Literacy – national survey data

- Student Academic Performance – using performance on state test

- School Quality – using state rating system

- Equity in Education – using race/ethnic disparities among top rated schools

- Equity in Law Enforcement - race/ethnic disparities in justice system

- Equity in Access to Capital – using race/ethnic disparities in loan rejections

---

[1] This word is capitalized throughout the text to emphasize its collective significance, like County.

- Equity in Leadership Positions – using race/ethnic/gender disparities in civic and business leadership

- Participation in the Arts – using percent attending two or more activities

- Philanthropy and Volunteerism – using incidence of volunteering/giving

- Neighborliness – using percent comfortable asking a neighbor for help/favor

- Quality of child care – using turnover rate of child care workers

- Access to child care – using number of subsidized child care spaces

- Civic Engagement – using percent voting in local elections by registered voters

While these measures have only recently become available, think through the history of the Branom Community and consider how well this Community has rated through the years, in its pioneer years, its glory years and its declining years.

First, we look at the history of governments who claimed ownership of the territory in the area. Next, we identify the people who came and settled the area. A classification of the settlers' information is borrowed from the Lamar County Historical Association's classifications beginning with the old Red River District. For example, settlers in Texas before the close of the year 1830 would be classed as **Pathfinders**, while those who came between that date and the close of the year 1850 would be classed as **Pioneers**. Those coming after the close of the year 1870, would be regarded as **old settlers**. (Ed H. McCuistion, October, 1995) Instead of restricting this system to the Red River District, I am applying the classification system to settlers in general who came to the territory that became Texas. In addition, anyone who came after the close of 1870, I am simply calling, '**Settlers**.' From this point, we distinguish those families who moved on from those who stayed by referring to them as settlers vs. searchers, and begin to mark the decline of the Community that was established over time.

In the pioneer days, the forts were hubs of civilization while the churches took over as people settled and safety from the Indians became less of a threat. Initially, the Mexican government insisted that new settlers to Texas take on of be of the Catholic faith, even thouogh most were protestants. When they moved, if they were a people of faith, they brought it with them. Whether Catholic or protestant, they were predominately Christians.

Take making a decision about which church to attend as an example of discerning what it means to be a searcher or a settler (or a pioneer – at least describing the 'attitude' of a pioneer) especially when it comes to finding a 'smaller church'.

The smaller church typically is at a place, size-wise, where there is not yet a big enough nucleus to have a youth group, or a young adult ministry, or a praise band, or a _____ (fill in the blank).

When a family with young children or middle school/high school children visits the smaller church without _____ (fill in the blank), it is understandable that they might wonder, "Is this the best place for us and our children?"

How We View Life Matters

How we answer that question depends on many variables, including our view of our family, our family's calling, and what type of upbringing best prepares young people for a Christ-like life of service to others.

If our view of life is, "My kids need the best of everything to survive in life," then we will make church choices based on that.

On the other hand, if our view of life is, "We are called to model and teach a life of sacrificial service for others which will prepare our children (and others) to thrive in adulthood," then we will make church choices of a very different type.

Ask yourself: What truly prepares us for real life as real Christians?

Given that:

- life out there is very hard: does it really prepare our kids for the real world when their church life is very easy?

- Christ calls us to sacrifice for others: does it really prepare our kids for Christian living in the real world when our church-shopping choices are all about what is best for us? Or, given

- life out there is very hard: is it possible that what best prepares our kids (or us) for the real world is a "pioneer" mindset about church life?

The Pioneer spirit can simply be defined as a willingness

to endure hardship in order to explore new places or try out new the pioneering spirit of the Americans as they pushed and fought their way from the east to the west coast of their continent. This pioneering spirit of our ancestors took them to many other lands.

Think about the Pathfinders in Hopkins County and the Branom Community. They risked their lives and moved into a virgin area and made a home—a settlement—long before they had any comforts of home. http://www.rpmministries.org/wp-content/uploads/2014/01/little-house-on-the-prairie.jpg

Then, others moved into that settlement—and benefitted from the sacrifices that pioneer families had made.

When the next generation of kids in that settlement town grew up, which ones do you think were tougher? Were better prepared for real life? Were able to live a sacrificial, Christlike life?

Was it the folks who came *after* the hard work of the settlement was done? Doubtful—those kids would have been more pampered in life, so they were likely easily discouraged by life.

Instead, don't you think it was kids of the pathfinder kids who were best prepared for real life? They knew what it was to grow up as pioneers—who worked hard, who sacrificed, who built something that others could benefit from.

The Pioneer Community Mindset

In church, Community and real life, especially with the smaller church and a smaller Community, what's needed is a pioneer mindset.

A family enters a church. They see that it's "small." And they recognize that there's not a larger enough nucleus *yet* to start a children's ministry, or a youth group, or a worship band, or a young adult's marriage group, or a _____ (fill in the blank).

That family with young kids or pre-teen kids just about decides to leave. Then they think of the Pathfinders. They stay. They sacrifice. They build a settlement *for others to benefit from*.

More importantly, they think of Christ. They "fix their eyes on Jesus, the pioneer and perfecter of faith. For the joy set before him he endured the cross, scorning its shame, and sat down at the right hand of the throne of God" (Hebrews 12:2).

What if we made choices that were for the eternal benefit of our descendants (or others)? What if we made choices that reflected Christ's pioneer mindset? Choices where we taught them that, "We're going to be pioneers in this world. There's no settling for less, so we will be the first, the pioneers. Others can come later and benefit from our sacrifice. And is it even that big a sacrifice since Christ, the true Pioneer, endured the cross for us!?" (Kellemen 2014)

When you read a name on the following pages, pause for a moment and whisper the name aloud and breath life into a voice long silenced. Spread throughout the pages that follow are brief life stories of people and, in some cases, their families who helped form and shape the Branom Community in western Hopkins County, Texas. Ponder whether or not you sense a pioneer's life as you read the story that brings that person back to life for you.

As with previous histories of any area, there is usually a subjective slant. In the case of this history, an attempt has been made to provide objective, factual information about who the first settlers were and their contribution to the area. The content of this work is not a genealogy of the area, but does include genealogical information and sources from Ancestry.com are <u>not</u> routinely documented. Families are mentioned as they appear being documented on the scene. Their services to the Community are mentioned as documented in prior histories, church records, military records, and government records. The sources are also included for the researcher who wants to investigate further. Hopefully, this work will help preserve that history for future readers.

– Billy D. Haddock

1 PATHFINDERS – before the close of 1830

Early Explorers

The **first** stage of frontier settlement is the *exploration* by European expeditions of the territory beyond the frontier. From Dr. Rex Strickland's book, entitled: *Red River Pioneers*, we learn that the Spanish explored Northeast Texas as early as 1687 and maybe as early as the mid-1500s. With one exception, most were traveling through on expeditions. The exception was Nacogdoches. The French also explored the area. Most of the accounts of these trips involved describing the countryside, including the rivers, and talking about the native Americans.

Indians

The **second** stage of settling the frontier was the *development of contacts* between trappers and missionary, on the one hand, and the native population, on the other. Reverse the point of view for a moment and consider what it was like from the native American perspective.

Here is a somewhat humorous accounting, supposedly by an Indian chief's response to a government official's question about what went wrong: "When white man find land, Indians running it, no taxes, no debt, plenty buffalo, plenty beaver, clean water. Women did all the work, Medicine man free. Indian man spend all day hunting and fishing; all night having sex. Only white man dumb enough to think he could improve a system like that."

The increasingly frequent appearance of odd-looking strangers who arrived in ever greater numbers along their shores was troubling. Most times these strangers seemed just to be looking around, exploring the coastline and various river inlets. Other times they seemed interested in trading, often wonderful things, for items that the Indians traditionally traded among themselves. The Native American culture had no concept of land ownership. To trade anything for land ownership was a ludicrous idea to them, so they gladly traded, thinking they had made a good deal.

Sometimes the invaders came wrapped in metal and carrying loud, deadly sticks that could kill a man at a long distance; frequently they took away women and children never to be seen again. And what was worse, shortly after the appearances of these strangers, people in the villages became sick and a great many died.

Many tribes adjusted to the invasion with a 'live and let live' attitude. Some even helped them survive the harsh winters. That was until the invaders started pushing them out of their native lands and destroying the hunting prospects. To make matters worse, they kept coming! If the Native Americans resisted and attacked, the white invaders banded together and used their superior weapons against them.

By the time settlers reached Texas, many tribes had already been pushed west, out of their native lands. The more civilized tribes had gradually adapted to the new culture. Others simply became more radical in their opposition to the invasion.

Though originally inhabited by the Caddo, and later Cherokee Indian tribes, the first evidence found of settlement by white pioneers was 1837. After the Caddos were displaced by the Cherokees, local Indian raids began to diminish because the

Cherokees were more civilized and, with that, religious and peaceful. However, a new threat emerged by way of the Comanches, a warring, nomadic tribe who were prone to steal, murder, rape, and kidnap unprotected pioneers, then ride for days to get away from retaliation. While the white man's technology was a superior weapon, the Comanche had their own technology, the Spanish mustang. They were <u>not</u> prone to be religious or practice many rituals at all. This group continued to terrorize Texans well past the Civil War and reconstruction periods.

Independence from Spain: Timelines

1821 - With the signing of the Treaty of Cordoba, Mexico is free from Spanish control after 300 years as a Spanish colony and 11 years of revolution.

Colonization Laws

1823 - Mexico passes the General Colonization Law, formally opening Texas to colonization. Presenting empresario[2] grants to individuals, the hope is to encourage settlement and economic growth in the remote Mexican land of Texas. An unstated motivation of the Mexican government was to provide a buffer between the Comanche Indians and Spanish settlements in what would become Texas and New Mexico.

Mexican Constitution of 1824

1824 - The Mexican government adopts the Constitution of 1824. Based on the United States constitution, Texians are, for the most part, in favor of the document. Texas and Coahuila are joined as a

---

[2] Spanish for entrepreneur.

single Mexican state.

Manuel de Mier y Teran

1828 - Mier y Teran is sent on a fact-finding mission to Texas by the Mexican government. Because of U.S. interest in Texas and the large number of Anglo settlers flowing into Mexico, the government is anxious to assess the situation.

1829 - In his report to the Mexican government, Mier y Teran recounts that the Americans living in the Nacogdoches area outnumber Mexicans 10 to 1 and American influence is apparent throughout Texas.

Mexican Soldiers

1830 - In response to Mier y Teran's report, the Mexican government enacts the Law of April 6th. This law prohibits the immigration of any more Americans into Texas, places taxes on goods coming into Texas from the U.S., prohibits slaves from entering Texas from the U.S., and deploys Mexican troops for permanent duty station in Texas. The year before Mexico had abolished slavery altogether.

Presidente Bustamente

1832 - In June, Anglo-American settlers rebel against the Bustamente government and its violations of the Mexican Constitution of 1824. They adopt the Turtle Bayou Resolutions, pledging support for the constitution and urge all Texians to support the patriots fighting under Santa Anna to defeat military despotism.

1832 - In October, Texians convene in San Felipe de Austin for the Convention of 1832; they organize municipalities and adopt a series of resolutions, the most controversial being a request for separate statehood from Coahuila. The Mexican government claims the meeting is unauthorized and illegal and does not recognize the resolutions.

Presidente Santa Anna

1833 - Texians convene in April in San Felipe de Austin for the Convention of 1833. Delegates write a state constitution for Texas and send Stephen F. Austin to Mexico City with a petition for statehood. Their countrymen elect Santa Anna as the Federalist president of Mexico.

American history reveals that in the 1820's settlers from Tennessee, Kentucky, Arkansas and Missouri moved to Texas. These were mostly yeoman farmers driven by the Mexican government's policy instituted to attract settlers. Americans were welcomed into the region as stabilizing the border, but the result was a Texas, rapidly turning into an American province. The total population on the eve of the Texas revolution, in 1835, was about 35,000 people. During the 19th century (1800s) there were streams of migration into Texas. Between 1821 and 1836 an estimated 38,000 settlers, on promise of 4,000 acres (1,620 hectares) per family for small fees, trekked from the United States into the territory.

Empresarios: Settlement Managers

Moses Austin was one of the early empresarios, followed by others, such as Stephen F. Austin, Green DeWitt, Haden Edwards, and Martin de León, who found the areas around the Brazos, Colorado, and Trinity Rivers to be especially hospitable, and soon fledgling colonies sprung up in eastern and central Texas.

Arthur G. Wavell and Ben Milam

Arthur Goodall Wavell, English soldier of fortune and colonial empresario, was born in Edinburgh, Scotland, on March 20, 1785, the son of William Wavell. He attended Winchester College from 1798 through 1804 and began his military career on April 10, 1805. In July 1820 he joined the revolutionary Chilean army as colonel of an infantry regiment. After reaching the rank of major general and deputy commander of the army, he was sent to Mexico as a special aide. There he accepted a commission as a brigadier general in the Mexican army and was quickly promoted to major general. In Mexico he published textbooks on infantry and cavalry tactics and a code of regulation as well as several pamphlets on the defense of various regions of the country. While he was in the Chilean service Wavell had met Moses Austin and developed an enthusiasm for his colonization scheme in Texas. With the death of the elder Austin, Wavell helped Stephen F. Austin transfer the empresario grant to his name. Wavell gave Austin a room in his apartments, and the two men agreed to join forces and share equally in the profits from the Austin Colony. Years later Wavell "boldly affirm[ed] that but for [his] aid both pecuniary, & in his Papers, & urging men in Power to advance his claims . . . his Grant the Cradle of Texas would never have been obtained."

1822 - Austin granted Wavell his power of attorney to form a company in England for the development of his Texas colony. Austin's land grant and such capital as Wavell might raise were to be the joint stock. Although the terms of the agreement for raising funds for Austin's colony had never been put into effect, Wavell still had claims against Austin for loans made to him in 1822, and in 1826 he appointed Benjamin Rush Milam as his agent to recoup his investment. No money, however, was ever recovered.

1824 - Wavell wrote to Austin for advice on his own colonization efforts. Austin responded in wholly negative terms. "I am heartily sick of the whole business," he informed his former partner, and advised him that if he wished "to keep out of trouble let colonization matters alone, either here or anywhere else." Nevertheless, on July 30, 1825, Wavell applied for a grant between Sulphur Fork and Kiamichi River on the Red River, an area recommended by Milam that Wavell himself had never seen. On March 9, 1826, the vice governor of Coahuila and Texas, Ignacio de Arispe, granted Wavell's request, giving him a six year time limit to complete the colonization of what is now Lamar, Red River, and Bowie counties as well as portions of Fannin and Hunt counties and Miller County, Arkansas. Wavell's efforts to promote the colony in England were fruitless, however, and Milam's attempts to draw colonists from the United States were hampered to a large degree by Mexico's hostility to slavery, without which the production of cotton was next to impossible. Too, the great Red River Raft, a log jam stretching 165 miles from Loggy Bayou to Carolina Bluffs, prevented river transport to and from the colony. The United States disputed the eastern border of the Wavell grant, correctly claiming that it was actually within the southwest boundary of Arkansas, and finally, on April 6, 1830, Mexico banned further immigration from the United States and refused to issue land titles to any of the colonists that Milam had recruited.

1826 - Wavell attempted to visit his colony but was prevented by flood waters. In 1828 he returned to Mexico, but did not visit Texas, and in 1831 an attack of rheumatism stopped him from viewing his grant. With Milam's death at the siege of Bexar in 1835, colonization efforts came to a virtual standstill. In 1837 Wavell divided his share in the grant with Milam's heirs, and only in 1841 was the survey of the grant completed.

Stephen F. Austin

1834 - Stephen F. Austin is arrested and imprisoned in Mexico City. Though accused of trying to incite insurrection in Texas, no charges are made against him, no court will accept jurisdiction of his case, and he remains a prisoner, shifting from prison to prison, from January until December 1834, when he is released on bond.

1834 - Santa Anna becomes dictator of Mexico, replacing the Federalist government with a Centralist government and disregards the Constitution of 1824.

1835 - The first governing body of Texas, the Permanent Council, acts decisively as it awaits a quorum for the November Consultation at San Felipe: it creates a postal system, plans for the Navy, and requests a loan from the United States. When the Consultation convenes, it adopts a revised constitution and creates a provisional government.

Philip Haddox, alias Coe, was one of five men representing Washington County in the Consultation. Also, he was one of the earliest taxpayers. His name appears on the list of 1837. Remember, he was a fugitive from Georgia!

Feb 29, 1836 - William Fairfax Gray, a Virginia land agent who traveled to Texas in 1836 searching for land deals, recorded some of Texas' most historic moments in a diary. His daily entries give a look into the tension and turmoil he witnessed at the Convention of 1836.

On this day, he writes, "A warm day, threatening rain from the south. Many other members are coming in, and it is now evident that a quorum will be formed tomorrow."

Dawn of the Signing: Texas Independence

March 1, 1836. The Fourth Convention is held at Washington-on-the-Brazos. It will declare independence, write a constitution for the new Republic, and elect an ad-interim government that controls Texas until regular elections can be held in the fall. "Notwithstanding the cold, the members of the Convention,....met today in an unfinished house, without doors or windows. In lieu of glass, cotton cloth was stretched across the windows, which partially excluded the cold wind."

Mar 2, 1836. "Mr. Childers, from the committee, reported a Declaration of Independence, which he read in his place. It was received by the house...and unanimously adopted, in less than one hour from its first and only reading."

Mar 3, 1836. Convention delegates sign the Texas Declaration of Independence. This document draws heavily on the Declaration written sixty years earlier by Thomas Jefferson. It proclaims that the Mexican government "ceased to protect the lives, liberty, and property of the people, from whom its legitimate powers are derived" and complains about "arbitrary acts of oppression and tyranny". The declaration officially establishes the Republic of Texas.

Mar 6, 1836. From Gray's diary: "This morning, while at breakfast, a dispatch was received from Travis, dated Alamo, March 3. The members of the Convention and the citizens all crowded to the Convention room to hear it read, after which Mr. Potter moved that the Convention organize a provisional government and adjourn and take the field."

In a separate letter to Jesse Grimes, also dated March 3rd, Travis states, "Let the Convention go on and make a declaration of independence, and we will then understand, and the world will understand, what we are fighting for. If independence is not declared, I shall lay down my arms, and so will the men under my command."

March 1836. Lorenzo de Zavala plays a key role in the Constitutional Convention of 1836. He is unanimously elected to serve as Vice President of the Republic of Texas. Zavala proposes a resolution that the constitution and laws of Texas be translated into the Spanish language.

Mar 7, 1836. "The Convention proceeded to work on the Constitution. It is reported in part only. Mr. Thomas is the chairman, or organ of the committee who reported. It is awkwardly framed, arrangement and phraseology both bad."

Mar 16, 1836. "The Constitution not being quite ready, they adjourned to 10 o'clock. At 12 o'clock the Constitution was finally adopted.... An ordinance organizing a provisional government was then adopted, consisting of President, Vice President, four Secretaries, and an Attorney General.... The new officers were sworn in at 4 o'clock in the morning, and the Convention adjourned until tomorrow."

Runaway Scrape

This term was the name Texans applied to the flight from their homes when Santa Anna began his attempted conquest of Texas in February 1836. The first communities to be affected were those in the south-central portions of Texas around San Patricio,

Refugio, and San Antonio. The people began to leave that area as early as January 14, 1836, when the Mexicans were reported gathering on the Rio Grande. When Sam Houston arrived in Gonzales on March 11 and was informed of the fall of the Alamo, he decided upon retreat to the Colorado River and ordered all inhabitants to accompany him. Couriers were dispatched from Gonzales to carry the news of the fall of the Alamo, and when they received that news, people all over Texas began to leave everything and make their way to safety. Houston's retreat marked the beginning of the Runaway Scrape on a large scale. Washington-on-the-Brazos was deserted by March 17, and about April 1 Richmond was evacuated, as were the settlements on both sides of the Brazos River. (Covington 2010)

Mar 17, 1836. "The [Convention] members are now dispersing in all directions, with haste and in confusion." —William Fairfax Gray (www.txindependence.org page 9)

President Sam Houston

October 1836 - In early October, the first Congress convenes in Columbia. At the end of the month, Sam Houston defeats Stephen F. Austin to become the first regularly elected President of Texas. He works to demilitarize Texas, establish peace with the Indians, and annex Texas to the United States.

1837 - The Republic of Texas is officially recognized by the United States, and later by France, England, the Netherlands and Belgium. In **1829,** the Guerrero decree conditionally abolished slavery throughout Mexican territories. It was a decision that increased tensions with slaveholders among the Anglo-Americans. After the Texas Revolution ended in **1836**, the Constitution of the Republic of Texas made slavery legal and it was passed in 1837.

Mirabeau Lamar

1838 - After serving as Sam Houston's vice president, Mirabeau Lamar succeeds Houston as President of the Republic of Texas. His greatest contribution to Texas is his vision for an educational system endowed by public lands. In addition, while Houston tried to make and keep peace with the Indians, Lamar worked toward moving the Comanches out of Texas.

Jan 25, 1839 - The Republic of Texas adopts its new flag (Museum 2017)

The names and geography of Hopkins County, Texas

To understand the geography and lay of the land is to understand it's history. Remember that Hopkins County was part of Lamar County before 1846. So, when thinking about the places of residence during the Texas independence period and following, Hopkins County was referred to as Red River County in 1837, shortly after winning independence from Mexico and, then, named Lamar County in 1841. It was 1846 before it became Hopkins County.

The first Anglo settlers in that area were in the Northeastern part of Red River County between 1816-1820. There were about four families. One day while the men were out hunting, Indians attacked the settlement and killed the women, children and slaves. The men pursued and were also killed. So, that settlement was just temporary. Jonesboro was the first permanent settlement in that area.

Looking at a present-day map, Hopkins County is bordered by Delta County to the north, Franklin County to the east, Hunt County to the west, and Wood & Rains County to the south. The terrain of Hopkins County is level to rolling, and its elevations range from 350 to 650 feet above mean sea level. The higher elevations form a divide east-to-west along what is roughly the center of the County. North of the divide the small streams flow north, and south of the divide, south.

The County's major interior stream, White Oak Creek, traverses the east-west center of the County, heading slightly to the northeast. The climate is humid and subtropical, with an average rainfall of 45 inches a year. Temperatures range from an average low of 32° F in January to an average high of 95° F in August. The growing season averages 238 days a year.

As stated, the area that became Hopkins County was originally occupied by the Caddo Indians, who were later displaced by the Cherokees. Troops dispatched by the Republic of Texas under the command of Gen. Kelsey H. Douglass defeated the Cherokees in 1839. This event encouraged settlers, now relatively free from Indian attacks, to move south into what is now Hopkins County. A grave marker near the first white settlement in that part, Sulphur Bluff, verifies the claim that settlers were in the area by 1837. (Harlin 2016)

In the 1830's, the area now known as Cumby, already had the name of Blackjack Camping Ground because of the blackjack oak trees. The main reason the area made such a good camping ground was that it is located at the highest elevation above sea level in Hopkins County. Originally, the Indians would bring their families with them into this area and set up camp. Therefore, the people of the Branom Community and its history has its beginnings under the name of Black Jack Grove.

Rangers & Forts

The **third** stage of frontier settlement is *building up forts and settlements* and further exploration of the territory. During the early years of the Republic of Texas, County residents lived in constant danger of Indian attack, and forts were a frequent refuge for settlers on the western edge of the Red River frontier.

Loosely organized ranger companies operated as early as 1823. Rangers were a group of armed men who operated independently from a regular military organization. They were generally self-armed, non-uniformed squads of civilians who patrolled the outer frontiers of a settled area to protect against Indian hostilities. Stephen F. Austin first used the term. People settled in certain areas during those days because there was protection from the hostiles nearby, along with water, good hunting and fertile farming land. This was an underlying economic fear that fueled and motivated the early pathfinders. They sacrificed the conveniences of religion, education, and the established protection found in more civilized and settled area.

Like all animals, humankind uses the same protective mechanisms either by isolating and making sure necessities were available in good supply; or pairing up, often with a stronger other, including choosing a mate from a hearty pathfinder family, or grouping up, such as banding together with other families, herding in protective areas, like forts and other settlements, or coming together in local militias for short periods of time to fight Indians, search for, catch, and punish thieves. Each of these methods were used effectively as often as possible during these times.

Even on the official Texas Ranger website, we learn that it is often difficult in the pre-Civil War era to separate the ranging companies, often functioning as a militia, from purely military units - and in some cases the ranging companies were attached to the military and reported to military commanders. The first of what appears to be a legally authorized ranger company included that of Captain Philip Haddox Coe[3] on July 9, 1835. His 12-man unit was considered to be 'Rangers under the command of Col. John H. Moore.'

1838-1839 Rangers were operating in the Lamar County (which included Hopkins County at the time) and Houston County area. The men often served for 3-month periods of time. Many were single, but others were married and had families, so they didn't want to be away for extended periods of time.

Early forts along the Red River were Ft. Johnson, Ft. Washita, Ft. Lyday and Ft. Inglish, near Bonham, and Ft. Shelton, near Paris, which was like many early forts, a fortified home, housing with protected walls surrounding it, within sound and sight of the fields where residents worked on crops. Between Paris and Clarksville was Ft. Towson. As settlers moved south, Ft. Houston was established in Houston County near present day Crockett and Ft. Parker, near present day Mexia.

Other forts in the area established later were: Ft. Belknap, Ft. Worth, Fort Dodge and Fort Leavenworth in Kansas.

Indians in the Republic of Texas

There were many Indians living in Texas during the time of Texas independence. Most significant were the Comanches and

---

[3] He changed his last name from Haddox to Coe after he escaped legal charges from Georgia to Texas in the 1820's.

Kiowas. They operated under the commands of Chief Big Tree and Chief Santana as early as the 1830's around Northeast Texas. **Santana was born around 1820, probably in what is now Kansas or Oklahoma.** However, it wasn't until 1836 that people began to realize how big a problem they really were.

It was publicized with the Parker massacre in May 1836 when the Comanches attacked the Parker family at Fort Parker near present day Mexia, without any warning and killed and kidnapped several members of the family. The, now famous, Cynthia Ann Parker was the most known. Rachel Parker Palmer, who was also taken captive, journaled her experiences in detail, giving the rest of the pioneers a glimpse into the barbaric practices of these tribes.

The Mexican government, and before them, the Spanish, knew. However, they weren't sharing information with the Texas settlers. From G.C. Gwynne 's book, *Empire of the Summer Moon*, we learn these governments may have been using Texas pioneers to create a buffer between them and the Comanches.

The Spanish knew that the Comanches had developed from a dull, primitive tribe to a strong, vengeful, clever people from 1625 to the mid-1750's, through adapting and using the horse, brought over from Spain. Without the mustang, a desert horse, they probably would have remained Stone Age hunters. By the early 1600's, wild mustangs had spread all the way up to what is now, New Mexico.

Apaches were raiding in New Mexico by the mid-1650's and all Indians in Texas had horses by 1700. Horses were the new technology of that time. However, the Comanches were the only tribe to learn to fight from horseback. And they became experts at it.

Because of their expertise, they developed a striking range for raids up to 400 miles. They were difficult to catch when they would ride into an area where no Indians lived, raid, kill, rape, mutilate, and run away with captives and livestock by riding all night and keeping so much distance between their camp and their victims. They were also good traders, selling buffalo hides, stolen horses, and captives then buying guns, ammunition, and food.

The Comanches stalled migration of Texas settlers for several years after it became a republic all the way past the Reconstruction period. The border was, essentially where the wooded land ended, and the Texas prairies began. This would be around Ft. Worth, south to Waco, then westward past San Antonio.

Consequently, some people settled in East Texas and didn't move west until later, if at all. People who did move were like the PARKER family: Calvinistic, righteous, hard-nosed, and audacious. Some said they were God-fearing people and had little fear left over for the Indians. Taken as a child, Cynthia Ann became integrated into the Comanche band and married, having at least two children. When first found living among the Comanches and given a chance to leave, she declined.

In 1839, a band of Comanche Indians came through the Black Jack Grove area to nearby Mt Vernon in Franklin County, then murdered and scalped a family. A company of Texas Rangers were then stationed near present day Daingerfield. When they heard of the depredation of the Indians, the rangers went in pursuit of them. Nearing the grove of Blackjack trees, they saw that the Indians had scattered in different directions in order to throw the

Rangers off their trail. The Rangers stopped at the old camping ground they knew (Black Jack Grove). While there, one ranger became sick and died in a few days. They buried him in the woods, a little north of the camp. A grave there was dug into a few years before 1934. Since no marker exists for this grave, it is thought to be the same grave of the aforementioned Ranger.

As we turn the focus to early settlers, we begin with the residents who helped protect the area since they were instrumental in helping provide safety to a sparsely populated area. You will note that most of them served in their young and single days, electing to stay and protect their families, once married. Some, who were older, had previous military experience. The younger ones would, later, fight in the Civil War. Others served as local sheriffs and other forms of law enforcement.

Early Settlers

All those who came to the old Red River District (in Texas) before the close of the year 1830 are classed as **Pathfinders**. (Ed H. McCuistion, October, 1995)

Some are obvious and have already been mentioned, as they played an active role in helping Texas obtain its independence. Others were more obscure and simply came to establish their familes in the area.

Using this system, we find **Pathfinders** (before the close of the year 1830), such as:

About 1816 - Benjamin Rush Milam was born in Kentucky about 1788 and fought in the War of 1812. By 1818 he was in Texas trading with the Comanche Indians on the Colorado River. In New Orleans in 1819 Milam met men who were planning an expedition to help the revolutionaries in Mexico and Texas gain independence from Spain. Milam joined with these friends who had similar goals and ended up imprisoned in Mexico City. Through the influence of Joel R. Poinsett, United States minister, all were released.

By the spring of 1824 Milam returned to Mexico, which now had adopted the Constitution of 1824 and had a republican form of government. In Mexico City he met Arthur G. Wavell and ended up dying in the campaign of Bexar[4] in November 1835. He is buried in Milam Park in San Antonio, Texas after his remains were dug up and moved at least two times. He was a Mason.

1816 – William Ragsdale, Jr. Born in Virginia, he and his family flat-boated to Texas from Kentucky, after returning from the War of 1812. William and family moved in 1816 to Texas with the Milan Colony, arriving in 1818, in old Miller County, Arkansas, now Texas. They had 88 grandchildren who were eventually dispersed throughout Texas, including relatives in the Branom community through niece, Rebecca Ragsdale (**my 4ᵗʰ great-grandmother**), who married into the Thomas Yates family.

The Ragsdales, as a family, were early immigrants to the Kiamichi sector south of Red River, Texas. It was called Miller County, Arkansas back then. William, Jr. was a Mason.

1829 - Philip Haddox, alias Coe, was born in South Carolina and escaped prosecution in Georgia, changed his name to Philip Alexander (Haddox) Coe and married soon after arriving in Texas. He was a fugitive, wanted for murder in Georgia and probably changed other facts about himself, also. For example, he claimed

---

[4] Also called the siege of Bexar.

he was from Alabama, where his dad's brother, Wm M, lived. His descendants married into the Pipkin family. He first, settled near Brenham in Washington County. Later, he homesteaded 4,446 acres of land northeast of Gonzales. He is listed among the 1st 300 Register of Families in Austin's Colony.

Some ancestors ended up living in Hopkins County and are buried in the Mt. Zion cemetery, although his direct descendants settled around Gonzales County.

Bef. 1830 – Finley family. The name is of Scottish origin and the people were probably Scots-Irish, migrating from Scotland, Ireland, then the United States. The patriarch of this family is David-I C. Finley. We will refer to him as David I in order to keep everyone straight. He was born in Virginia and married there, then moved to Kentucky and ended up in Indiana. They appeared to have lived between Indiana and Missouri, with Indiana being east of the Mississippi and Missouri west of the river. David-I had at least two sons who lived in Texas early on: Jesse and Edmond 'Ed' Finley.

It is thought that one of the old-time citizens of this part of the County was Edward Finley (or possibly Edmund), referred to hereafter as Ed-I. Ed-I, David Finley's third child, was born in Virginia in 1787, raised in Missouri, but moved a few miles west of Ridgeway[5] and lived a life that proved a benediction to all who knew him. He was considered honest, industrious, religiously inclined, and raised an admirable family of children. It was difficult to track his exact family since the name (both first and last) was spelled differently (Edward or Edmund) (Finley, Findley, Findlay,

---

[5] *It was named for a pioneer family named Ridgeway and because of its location on a drainage ridge between White Oak Creek and the Sulphur River.*

etc.). In addition, it seems everyone named all their children after siblings in their family-of-origin and repeated the pattern. This writer resorted to naming each separately (I, II, III, etc.) according to birth dates. He (Ed-I) is believed to be one of the earliest settlers in the Branom area. (J. E. Tuck undated) It is not known where Edmund (Ed-I) and his wife, Catherine are buried, but they were probably buried in the Wren cemetery, located just down the hill east of the Mt. Zion cemetery on the west side of Wren Creek. Reportedly, this was a rather large cemetery which was washed away by flooding in the past. (Rollins 2002)

Two of Ed-I's sons, <u>David and Lewis Finley,</u> are also listed among the early residents of this area. David (referred to as David-II) was born in Missouri and died in Hopkins County. He must have moved to Texas about 1845, since his first child born in Texas was reported born there at that time. He is buried in the Mt. Zion cemetery.

In his older years, we found what appears to be him (Ed-I) on the census living with his son, Lewis & Letticia Findley with them at age 65 and 63 near Cumby. Lewis, the youngest son of Ed-I Finley, was born in Missouri, but all their children were born in Texas. Lewis and his family moved to Cooke County, Texas later and moved his mother, Catherine, with him. It looks like Catherine, his mother, lived with him the rest of her life. He remarried there after his wife, Letticia, died.

Reportedly, Ed-I was buried at the Plunkett School house a few miles east of Cumby. (Tuck undated) Another report says he is buried in the Pleasant Grove cemetery near Cumby.

<u>Jesse Finley</u>, David-I Finley's fifth child, was born in Kentucky in 1792, married in Indiana and died in Missouri. He and his wife,

Rachel, had at least 10 children, with 7 boys. He is listed on the 1850 Census in Hunt County, Texas living with his wife and six remaining children and farming on land adjoining his son, William. In looking at Jesse's residence before that, it appears they lived a few years in Indiana near his father, David-I, before moving to Texas after his father died. His wife, Rachel, died after November 1850 and it appears Jesse moved back to Missouri around that time where he later died. While Jesse didn't stay in Texas, his children did.

Jesse and Rachel's children:

We find <u>William J. 'Bill' Finley</u>, the oldest son of Jesse Finley, residing in Texas at age 25 when he married Elizabeth SIMMONS in Hunt County. On the 1872 map of Hopkins County, a Wm. Finley shows as owning land between Branom and Cumby near the western border of the County. It looks like he was a brother of Ed and shows up on the records when he left Misssouri and married in Hunt County. This helps document the Finley family in this area who moved there from Missouri. (Pressler 1872)[6]

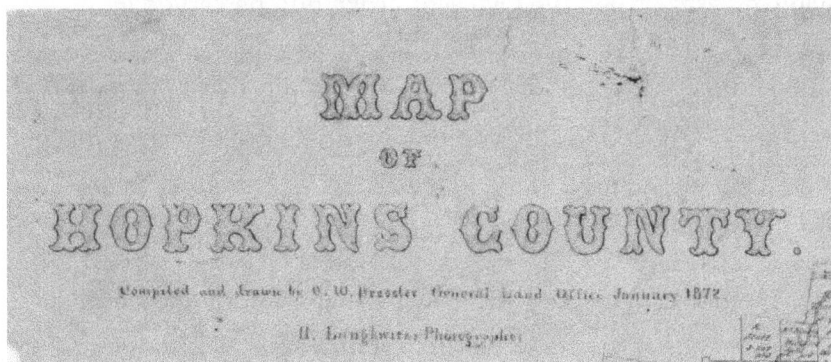

[6] accessed April 1, 2018), University of North Texas Libraries, The Portal to Texas History, texashistory.unt.edu; crediting Texas General Land Office.

From this, we are able to track his son, David M. Finley and wife, Phebe Hodges, who married in 1875 and had close ties with Mt. Zion. They buried four children, mostly infants, in Mt. Zion. One, Edmond T., provides additional clues since he was a twin. We can document his birth date from his brother, John William (Will), whom we know moved to Dallas where he was a practicing physician until his death.

Ed(II) Finley first appears on records living in Texas at age 23 with his parents, Jesse and Rachel, in Hunt County. He was born in 1827 in Indiana, lived in Missouri and didn't marry until he was living in Texas. When the Civil War broke out, he served in Company I, 23rd Texas Mounted Cavalry and the family later applied for a headstone for his service. He married in March 1863 to Mary KERBOW and survived the war to have children and lived to age 90. He is buried in the Pleasant Grove Cemetery near Cumby. After he died, his wife filed for a soldiers' pension.

Elizabeth Ellen Finley was the first daughter of Jesse and Rachel. After living in Texas a brief period, Merit Branom (another early settler) married Elizabeth 'Ellen' Findley, a sister to Ed (I) Finley and aunt to ex-tax assessor, Dave Finley. (www.accessgenealogy.com 2012)

It was written in the family Bible that he reportedly went back to Missouri to his old home and make her his wife, bringing her to Texas. In Missouri, the Finley family had already married into the Weir (Wear) family who were related to Laird Burns and his wife, Mary Polly Weir. All these families were prominent Cumberland Presbyterians.

Elizabeth Finley married Merit Branom on November 27, 1842, in Lamar County, Texas according to the marriage records. The 1872 map of Hopkins County, shows Merit Branom owned land just south of Sulphur River of what would be now called, Cooper Lake. They had 14 children in 20 years. She died in 1904 and is buried in the Cumby cemetery.

Their descendants married into the Young, Chaffin, McFarlin, Ward, Butler, Ingram, Gillis, Welch, Newell and Moore families. (www.accessgenealogy.com 2012)

Milton Finley was another of Jesse's sons. He married Orinda DAVIS on December 6, 1847 in Hopkins County. Her family had settled in Texas early and was thought to be part native American. In 1850, Harmon Blackmore (Orinda's uncle) and Joseph Proctor (Orinda's grandparent) families lived in Hopkins County on property in the same area as David II Finley, Milton's brother. Some of these families seem to have known each other dating all the way back to the Texas revolution.

It appears Milton's family lived in and around Sulphur Springs for a while.

In 1860, we did find his younger brother, William C. and sister, Catherine, living with him and his family. Those children must have stayed in Texas when their mother and father moved back to Missouri. Milton served in the Civil War and died around

1865, shortly after he married another woman who also was part Indian. The exact details of his death are still unknown at this time, but it is thought he moved to Darwin, Oklahoma (near Antlers) and is listed as dying there.

George Finley is the next son, who appeared on the records in Hunt County in March 1848 when he married Jane O'DELL, who was also from Missouri. On the November 1850 Census, he was found living in Hunt County farming on land adjoining his brother, Milton.

Joseph Jefferson (JJ) Finley was found living in Texas with his parents in Hunt County. He married at 27 to Nancy Jane 'Mary' SOUTHERLAND and moved to Sonoma County, California shortly after that where he lived until he died.

Marion Finley moved to Texas with his parents, married Arminda Kerbo in Hopkins County on April 17, 1862 and died in his early thirties.

Mary Elizabeth Finley also moved to Texas with her parents then married and died the same year, at age 22.

William C. and sister, Catherine Finley was last known to be living with their uncle Milton and his wife in 1860.

Summary for this period

In the early days, it appears that the recorded Pathfinders in Texas and the greater Red River County that ended up with descendents in the area were the Ragsdales and Haddox (alias Coe) families. In closer proximity to Branom, it was the Finley family who seem to have settled there prior to 1830 and were of Scots-Irish descent. Scots-Irish showed traits of loyalty, family pride, eagerness to fight, and self-sustainability, enduring traits that can be applied to many descendants of the Scots-Irish settlers. They are the men and women in rural areas, the soldiers, the hunters, the conservatives, the frugal, and the self-sustaining.

We see in the records that the Finley family lived in Missouri before moving to Texas. Since they settled early, they and their descendents will be referred to as an 'pathfinder family'.

When people moved to Texas, they often moved together with other families and settled close together for protection as much as for socialization, and the families intermarried. Also, during the early days, people were commonly introduced by where they were born, then from before moving to Texas. Of course, in the case of some people, like Philip Coe (Hattox) they may have lied to protect themselves. In other cases, it was just plain dangerous to ask too many questions.

Some pathfinders also married native Americans. As with Milton Finley, unions between whites and Indians were generally more accepted into Indian societies than white society. The offspring from white/Indian marriages often were more accepted by Indian, which usually meant membership in political and economic entities (i.e., tribes). The practical aspect meant that in order to be considered an Indian, one need to be at least one-quarter or more degree of Indian blood from that tribe to be a tribal citizen.

2 PIONEERS – 1831- 1850

According to Mexican law, slavery was illegal in Texas, but this area already had about 5,000 slaves at the time of its revolution in 1836. Indentured servitude was legal. The new republic made slavery legal in 1837, and by 1845, when the state was annexed to the United States, the number of slaves grew to 30,000. Texas applied for statehood just 16 years before the Civil War and was admitted to the Union in 1845 as a slave state.

The Texas Republic and early statehood

Pioneers, between 1830 and the close of the year 1850, were instrumental in settling this part of Texas. Some stayed while others moved on.

About 1830 - Edward H. Tarrant. From Wikipedia and Ancestry.com, we learn that he was a young veteran of the War of 1812, taking part in the Battle of New Orleans (1814–15) at the age of 19. He entered as a private and mustered out as a corporal in the Kentucky state militia. Having moved to Tennessee, he was elected a colonel of the Tennessee state militia, in the frontier environment. By 1827, Tarrant had become a sheriff of Henry County, Tennessee, in 1825 he helped organize the first Masonic lodge in Paris, Tennessee and in 1830, became postmaster; but he moved to Texas by the early 1830s and established a ranch in Red River County where he apparently opened his household to relatives, hired men, and slaves in Red River County, Texas, by November 23, 1835. On February 2, 1838, he received a league and labor of land from the Republic of Texas as part of a uniform grant made to all heads of families resident in Texas on March 2, 1836. Because of his prior service, he became a Brigadier General

28

of the Fourth Brigade of the Texas Militia and operated out of Ft. Johnson. He also served in the Rangers and as a chief Justice on the Texas Supreme Court. He became a prosperous landowner, owned slaves and, later, served two terms in the Texas legislature (3rd Texas Legislature). In 1847, Tarrant ran for lieutenant governor, but he was defeated by John Alexander Greer. Later in life, he moved to Ellis County, near Waxahachie. He built a house in 1845 and nearby he built the first mill in Ellis County. Here he resided until his death.

Ed McCuistion, once President of the Lamar County Historical Society, wrote the following about Tarrant, "He was a brilliant lawyer, a public-spirited man, (and) placed much in both a material and sacrificial way upon his County's altar." (McCuistion 1995)

The original County seat of Hopkins County was named after Tarrant, but later moved to what is now Sulphur Springs. Later, a Texas County was named after him and the County seat is Ft. Worth.

The Yates family. Three family members migrated into Texas early from Miller County, Arkansas which was just across River and even came down into Texas at the time. They were sons of Colonel Thomas Yates, Sr. and are listed below in order of documented residence:

1834 – Thomas Avis Yates, Jr. He was born in Tennessee. On 1 Feb 1838, he appeared before land commissioners for the Republic of Texas and took an oath that he was married and emigrated to Texas in 1834 and has been in Texas since. He fought with Ben

Milam[7] in the volunteer Texas army in the campaign of Bexar when they took San Antonio away from General Cos in the fall of 1835. Ben Milam was a fatality of that battle. Afterward, the volunteers returned to their farms to prepare for winter.

He is buried in the McDonald Cemetery, near Paris, Texas.

<u>1837 - William Thomas Yates.</u> He was a brother to Thomas Avis Yates, Jr. and filed for a land grant on the Lamar/Delta County line and received 644 acres. He is listed as one of the original landowners in Lamar County. Claims he was single when he came here (but married was marked through which could mean he was no longer married). Served in Stout's Company of Red River Rangers and worked out of Ft. Inglish and helped protect neighbors around Ft. Shelton and Roxton.

<u>1837 - George Yates.</u> He is number three of brothers who migrated into Texas early from Miller County, Arkansas. All are sons of Colonel Thomas Yates, Sr.

<u>1834 - William Griffin Yates</u>. While he was born in Tennessee, a younger brother was born in Texas In 1842 and he was most likely with his parents when they moved to Texas in 1834. He is the son of <u>Thomas Avis Yates, Jr.</u> and is listed as owning a large tract of land in Hopkins County on the 1872 map that has been mentioned.

Headright System attracted early settlers

In return for settling in Texas before its independence and for serving in the Texas volunteer army, Thomas Yates was granted 2

---

[7] *He was another Texas pathfinder and empressario who, along with Austin, helped attract settlers to the state.*

leagues of land (4,605 acres times 2). That land shows up on the map mentioned earlier as a big square with the following notations: No. 22, Thos Yates, N 1, 169. **He was my 3rd great grandfather.** Therefore, this writer went to the Hopkins County courthouse to research what happened with this land and found that the day after it was deeded to Thomas Yates by the state of Texas, it was sold the next day to a lawyer in Houston who sold it to another lawyer in New Orleans the next day. Selling price that Thomas Yates received: $1,000. In going through the related pages during that time, transactions like that were scattered throughout the ledger. It must have been a widespread practice of the times.

Beside Thomas A. Yates, there is another large tract of land patented in Hopkins County, that of William G. Yates, his son.

As stated, it looks like they primarily lived in Tennessee

before moving on to Texas.

Beside inexpensive land, there were two additional reasons people were attracted to migrate to Texas: <u>first</u>, through the 1820s, most believed that the United States would buy eastern Texas from Mexico. Many thought that that portion of Texas had been part of the Louisiana Purchase and that the United States had "given" it away to Spain in exchange for Florida in the 1819 Adams-Onís Treaty, which established the Sabine River boundary. The Texas pioneers expected annexation would stimulate immigration and provide buyers for their land. A <u>second</u> attraction was that Mexico and the United States had no reciprocal agreements enabling creditors to collect debts or to return fugitives. Therefore, Texas was a safe haven for the many Mississippi valley farmers who defaulted on their loans when agricultural prices declined at the end of the War of 1812 and bankers demanded immediate payment. Faced with seizure of their property and even debtors' prison in many states, men loaded their families and belongings into wagons and headed for the Sabine River, where creditors could not follow and there was opportunity to start over. The same was true for criminal fugitives from the law. Therefore, a central motivation for pioneers remained a desire for economic stability manifested in land ownership and a growing desire for educating their children and protecting them from threats to survival.

While it would be unfair to characterize Texas as a haven for heathens, it would be unrealistic to see it as a sanctuary for saints. (Brackenridge 1968) Families were encouraged to move to Texas, instead of single men, in order to promote a regard for stability. However, many of the early pioneers went with religious services and schooling of their children.

<u>1835 – Joseph Cromwell Matthews</u>. He was the patriarch of a large Tennessee family who immigrated to Texas in 1835. Before they died, they moved to what is now Rockwall or Kaufman County with one of their sons. Their graves were lost when the Rockwall Cemetery was destroyed.

Family legend has it that the Matthews family were friends of David Crockett and began the trip to Texas in his company.[8] Apparently, the wagon train moved too slowly for the eager men, for they left the group vowing to meet again in Texas. Upon arrival in Red River County, the Matthews set upon the task of preparing homes for their families. Several of the Matthews men joined the Texas Army and renewed their determinations for independence upon hearing of the deaths of their friends at the Alamo.

<u>Robert Evans Matthews</u> was a son who volunteered.

By 1846, the Matthews family was in Hopkins County where they, reportedly, owned large tracts of land. Robert Evans Matthews was the first County clerk, a position he held until 1858. After that, he moved to Cooke County where he lived until his death.

Robert's oldest child, was <u>Richard Hale Matthews</u> born in 1825 in Alabama. In 1847, he married and resided in Hopkins

---

[8] According to Crockett's history, their route was down the Mississippi River to the Arkansas and then up that river to Little Rock; then overland to Fulton, Arkansas, and up the Red River along the northern boundary of Texas; across the Red River, through Clarksville, to Nacogdoches and San Augustine; and on to San Antonio. At San Augustine the party evidently divided.

County. They lived in Parker and Cooke Counties, then returned to live in Hopkins County before they died.

1835 – Curtis C. Jordan – Here's what we know: He was Mary Elizabeth Ritchey's first husband having married her 12/30/1847. Records show his family living in Nacogdoches County, Texas in 1835. He is listed as living near David & Lewis Finley families on the 1850 Census farming about 500 acres in Hopkins County. He died in 1852 with cause of death unknown and she remarried a few years later.

As we move into the next chapter and learn about other early settlers in the Branom Community, reference will be made to land holdings on a County map made in 1872 to show approximately where people lived in reference to the South Sulphur River (a northern boundary) and Hunt County (a western boundary). (Pressler 1872)

For example, there is a C.C. Jordan listed on the map as a landowner with property located just southeast of the Sulphur River on that 1872 map. That would be near the Branom Community.

The first settlers of Hopkins County were, in the main, rural people and farmers, but they soon began to establish trading points in different parts of the County. Of course, Sulphur Bluff was the first, but at that time goods had to be hauled by ox wagon either from Shreveport on the Red River or from Little Rock on the Arkansas, which made merchandising almost prohibitive, and the settlers were left largely to their own resources. In 1845, it was found that boats could come up to the present site of Jefferson by following the channel of Cypress Bayou, and in a very short time Jefferson became the trading point for all northeast Texas.

On an old 1851 map, towns followed parallel to the Red River from Paris west to Honey Grove and Bonham and east to Clarksville and Boston (which became New Boston). That same road would now look like Highway 82, which extends to Denison, Sherman, and on west to Gainesville.

Stores were established at Sulphur Bluff; at the Black Jack Grove, now known as Cumby; at Tarrant, the first County seat of Hopkins County; Charleston near Cooper, in what is now Delta County, and possibly at other places - the ones named being established during the first fifteen years after the first settlement in the County. It will be noted that many of these trading points were in the south half of the County, but this was because the main Jefferson Highway and two of its branches penetrated this part of the County. Pickton, Weaver, and Ridgeway were established when the railroads were built. Accordingly, stores were also established, in Ridgeway, for example, when the railroad came through.

After Texas became a state in 1845, some individuals sought to represent the residents in state government. This was back when politicians were regular citizens who served temporarily, then resumed their regular occupations. Since many came for the land, their usual occupation was farming. During these days, people in Texas were often referred to by way of where they came from before migrating to Texas.

1836 - M.M. Green. Miller Green was born in Marion County, Texas, in March 1836, just a few days after the fall of the Alamo, with its band of brave defenders. Mr. Green moved to Hopkins County with his parents and located in Black Jack Grove on the corner that was afterwards known as the "Wharton place" on December 24, 1854, and Hopkins County was henceforth his home.

During the civil war, he was a member of Co. K, 9th Texas Cavalry, and saw much hard service with his regiment with Ross Cav celebrated brigade. He married a daughter of Wash Cole, a very prominent citizen of the County and a member of the State Legislature from Hopkins County in the early day. Mr. Green's father, Ben. F. Green, was in the war with Mexico, 1846 and 1847, and went with Taylor who crossed into Mexico at Matamoras.

His obituary: M. M. Green, a pioneer citizen of Hopkins County, died Tuesday night at his home in Cumby where he lived more than 83 years. Burial was made in Cumby. He was born near Daingerfield, but, with his family, moved to Hopkins County 68 years ago. He was a member of the Texas Rangers for two years and fought valiantly for the Confederate Army for four long years. He carried the chain when the town of Greenville was surveyed and was deputy sheriff when the County seat of Hopkins County was moved from Old Tarrant to Sulphur Springs. In fact, he is older than the State of Texas, having been born under the Republic of Texas before Texas became a State. He has lived in Cumby longer than any other man and has raised a family of splendid sons and daughters; his wife having already preceded him to the Great Beyond. The living children are as follows: D. H. Green, Perry Green, B. F. Green, Mrs. Flora Mathis, Miss Pearl Green and Miss Juanita Green. Green, Miller M. - b. 20 Mar. 1836, d. 11 Dec. 1919 (Hopkins Co. Echo, Dec. 12, 1919)

From the Hopkins Genealogical website, we found the following additional information:

"Miller Green, who lived at Black Jack Grove, is a native Texan. He was born in Red River district in the year 1837. Two years after his

birth his father moved into the vicinity of where Greenville in Hunt County is situated. In the year 1854 he moved to the Cumby area.

In the year 1867 Miller married Ophelia Cole, daughter of Wash Cole, an old pioneer and one of the first who came to Hopkins County. He was highly respected and esteemed by all of his acquaintances. His name is agreeably remembered as that of one of the leading personages of the County. Ophelia was born at Old Sulphur Bluff in the year 1845, She is dead now, and so is her father. Together, they had seven children living.

He was a Texas Ranger, and served his state as an Indian fighter for two years. He was a soldier in the Confederate army and saw hard service for four years. He served under General Ross in the Ninth Texas Cavalry, receiving a slight wound while in the discharge of his duty.

When he returned from the war he engaged in farming and stock raising, and was reasonably successful. He has always been in easy circumstances, meeting his obligations promptly. He has been a taxpayer in the County since and before his majority. He has encouraged the upbuilding of schools, and has been liberal in their support. He is ready at all times to give encouragement to any enterprise for the improvement of his Community, a good citizen, a debt-paying man and a Democrat."
(www.accessgenealogy.com 2012)

<u>1837 – Jesse Shelton</u>. The Jesse Shelton family, originally from Virginia and Kentucky, and, most recently, from Miller County, Arkansas (now Bowie County, Texas), was well-known around what became the Paris, Texas area (Roxton and Pin Hook). Jesse was known to be an Indian fighter and a settler in the area just north of the Red River since the 1820's. Migrated from Virginia to

Texas before Texas became independent. Described as a 'loyal, warm-hearted, southern man.' So, he would be referred to as Jesse Shelton of Miller County, Arkansas or … of Kentucky.

It was in Kentucky that he married Rachel Marrs, part Choctaw Indian.

After the land they homesteaded in present day Arkansas was deeded to the Indians by the government, he moved his family south of the Red River in 1837 and settled near Roxton. At age 15, his son, Eli Jenway Shelton, who was born in Miller County, Arkansas, became one of the first Texas Rangers from Red River/Lamar County, who served 12/19/1838-5/26/1839 under Capt. H. D. Stout as a private. He was thought to be a magnificent horseman, a bold and daring rider, and a courageous and fearless Ranger. (McCuistion 1995)

He worked out of Ft. Inglish, Ft. Lyday, near Bonham and Ft. Shelton, near Roxton. In 1846, he married Elizabeth Ann Yates, another pioneer family who settled near Paris. Later, he served with the confederates in the Civil War and on the state legislature.

The Sheltons intermarried with the Thomas Avis Yates family since they lived near each other. Later, ancestors of the same Yates family would settle and marry into families of the Branom Community.

1837 – James Frances Box. He was found in Texas, 22 Oct 1837, after his 18-year-old daughter, Lucinda died.

James married Jemima Babb on 15 Jan 1817 in, Madison, Alabama. She was born about 1800 in, Alabama. She died before

May 1826. James then married <u>Elizabeth Matthews</u>[9], daughter of <u>Joseph Cromwell Matthews</u> and <u>Penina Crisp</u> on 15 May 1826 in, Lawrence, Alabama. Elizabeth was born about 1809 in Madison, Alabama. She died in Aug 1850 in Titus County, Texas. She was buried in Texas. James married Jane Goddard on 10 Dec 1852 in Navarro, Texas. It appears they had no children together. So, we have the Box, Babb, Crisp and Goddard families intermarrying.

There was a Capt. <u>James E. Box</u> in the Houston County Rangers, March 1839 - October 1839 and a James F. Box, who served TX Ranger duty. We know that he and his family members served in the below capacity to guard the Red River County and nearby counties. Some have been documented, some have not. We did find James F. Box on the Red River list.

Miss Verona Ozora Box was born in Johnson Co, Texas on July 28, 1865. She died on Sept 9, 1936 in Lamoni, Iowa. As a young lady, she moved to Arapaho with her mother, Mrs. Sarah Hatley Matthews Box. Mrs. Box was born Aug 25, 1833 in Gibson County TN, and died on March 2, 1921 in Arapaho, Oklahoma.

1836 - <u>Mansil Walter Matthews</u>. He was a brother of John W. Matthews, both from South Carolina. Lamar County was created in December 1840 from Red River County and it was also one of the Texas frontier counties designated to have a minuteman company. Captain Mansil Walter Matthews, 35, was elected to command these men. Matthews, a large man of 275 pounds, was a preacher, doctor, and legislator born on Christmas Eve 1806 in

---

[9] The spelling of Matthews, like other surnames, usually suggests some illiteracy and auditory error, <u>or</u> a difference between the way Catholics and Protestants spelled it. Efforts were made to correct all spelling errors with surnames.

Kentucky. He preached and taught in Tennessee and Alabama until 1835, then he began a career as a physician and Disciples of Christ minister.

He arrived in Red River County on January 17, 1836. After settling his family and winning the March 17 election as representative from Red River County to the First Texas Congress, he joined the Texas army and served as a surgeon until July 1836. He was at the battle of San Jacinto and attended the wounded Gen. Sam Houston when Houston's soldiers brought Gen. Antonio López de Santa Anna to Houston as a captive. Matthews attended the first session of the Congress, which met from October 3 to December 22, 1836, but then resigned his seat, having been elected president of the Board of Land Commissioners of Red River County. He also represented Red River County in the House of the Seventh Congress (1842–43) and at the Convention of 1845. In addition to other military activities, he served with Company F of the Texas Rifles during the Mexican War.

Matthews was an influential preacher in Hopkins County from about 1844 to 1855. He bought and sold thousands of acres, witnessed the marriage of numerous couples, and was postmaster at White Oak from 1847 to 1850.

1837 - Henry G. McDonald. Reportedly, he moved to the Republic of Texas in 1837. Apparently for his service in the Texas army, he received a grant of 1,280 acres in Red River (now Lamar) County. This property was located in what was later known as the Pleasant Grove (now Howland) Community 10 miles southwest of Paris. The Robinsons joined him there a few years later. In an affidavit tentatively dated February 1863, Lewis Robertson (sic, #14 above) stated that he "knew [Dr.] McDonald since 1841.

<u>1849 - Thomas Wade Box.</u> He was first recorded in Texas when he married into the Matthews family in Hopkins County. This was the same family that his dad married in to with his second wife. Wade, as he was called, was born on March 10, 1821 in Lawrence County, Alabama.

He died on Jan 14, 1875 in Red River Station, Montague County, Texas. He served in Captain Ross's Regiment, Texas Mounted Vis. (9th Cal) in the Civil War and worked as a surgeon. Mrs. Box drew a widow's pension from the United States of America, Mexican War, certificate # 7014.

More Pioneers

<u>1839 - John W. Matthews</u>. Born in South Carolina in 1796, he married Sara in 1820. About 1839, he moved to Red River County, Texas, probably with his cousin James E., and by the mid-1840s, is living in Hopkins County, Texas, amid the Joseph C. Matthews family. In time, he settled in the far southwestern corner of the County, away from many of the other Matthews.

In early 1850, Matthews conveyed to his daughter, Mary Matthews Box, a gift of 200 acres. This deed was notarized by M. W. Matthews.

In 1853, he advertised in the "Clarksville Standard" for the lost headright certificate for 1/3 of a league of land that he obtained from Wilson E. Ewing, administrator of the Estate of Randolph DeSpain from Kentucky, then deceased. He was shot by the Mexican Army under Gen. Santa Anna, March 27, 1836 in Goliad, Texas while serving as a soldier in the Texas war for independence.

The land, referred to as Granny's Neck, also known as Old

Granny's Neck, was six miles southeast of Cooper and one mile west of State Highway 154 where the Bonham-Jefferson road crossed the South Sulphur River in south central Delta County. The area was settled in 1846 when Brigadier DeSpain, his wife, Narcissa, and their three daughters arrived from Tennessee to claim land awarded to that relative, Randolph DeSpain mentioned above, who had been killed with James Walker Fannin, Jr., at Goliad.

Apparently, Matthews and his committee were just trying to clear up the paperwork.

Their survey was situated on both sides of the road, a major thoroughfare for transporting cotton. Soon after they settled, the DeSpains built a bridge across the South Sulphur on the highest ridge of land in the vicinity. The new bridge, sturdy and high enough to escape flooding, made the road an even more popular trade route. More settlers joined the DeSpains, including Mary "Granny" Sinclair, matriarch of the Sinclair family, who raised goats on a neck of land that jutted into the South Sulphur River. The Community was named for her. The Granny's Neck school, established after the Civil War, had one teacher and enrolled thirty-two pupils in 1905. The school later moved to Pecan Grove.

Wilson E. Ewing was the administrator of the DeSpain's estate, but we have not found the connection between Ewing and Matthews. A daughter married a Ewing, but the exact connection is unclear.

On 2/9/1848, John W. Matthews was appointed the first postmaster of Black Jack Grove (Cumby). He lived 3 miles north of town and kept the mail in his residence. Mail was received once weekly by horseback.

John W. Matthews apparently died after May 1868, but before the 1870 census, probably in Hopkins County, Texas. In May 1868, he applied for the remaining 320 acres due him out of his Third-Class Land Certificate (arrival in Texas between October 1, 1837 and January 1, 1840).

Matthews citizens on the official Texas Rangers roster:

- Capt. James D. Matthews (March 1839 - June 1839 - Mounted Rangers)

- Capt. W. M. C. Matthews (1862 - Precinct No. 2, Cooke County, 21st Brigade, TST)

The following pioneers were listed as early settlers in and around Cumby (J. E. Tuck undated)

1849 - Redelium Lindley was another prominent and well-known citizen who was born in Polk County, Missouri, in 1835. In 1849, with his father, John (or Jahu) Lindley, he located on South Sulphur creek in Hopkins County. On the 1850 Census, they were living in the Peerless Community. At the age of 23 he married Miss SAYLE, a member of a prominent and wealthy family in Hunt County. Mr. Lindley early gave his attention to the cattle industry and soon became the owner of a large lot of cattle. He would sell and buy and as he made money would purchase blocks of land, and when he died, was one of the large land owners of the County, besides possessor of much other property. During the civil war, Mr. Lindley was detailed with a force to protect the frontier, but never saw service where actual hostilities took place. (www.accessgenealogy.com 2012)

Charles C. 'Charley' Cate was born in Tennessee but came to Texas at an early age and with his brother, Tom, engaged in the mercantile business in old Black Jack Grove. When a company (Company K, 9th Cavalry) of soldiers was organized here on July 5, 1861, he enlisted and spent four years in the Confederate Army.

After the company had organized by electing Jim Williams, Captain; Mose Bowen, 1st Lieutenant; Merit Branom, 2nd Lieutenant; and Charley Mount, 3rd Lieutenant. This man, Mount, was first cousin to Charley Cate.

Charley and his wife, Molly had one son who became a physician and practiced in Commerce.

1849 - N. B. (Bony) and Luther Waggoner were sons of Solomon Waggoner who moved from Missouri to near Blossom Prairie in 1839. Luther was born in Missouri in 1833, but Bony was born near Blossom sometime in the 1840's.

The family moved to Hopkins County in 1849, and, another son, Dan, who later moved out west and carved an immense fortune, was born also in Missouri. Solomon Waggoner is buried in a mile or two from Peerless. Luther is buried in Cumby, while Bony sleeps In the Pleasant Grove cemetery. Luther was a Confederate soldier during the 1860's.

1839 - James D. Matthews. Another Matthews, Capt. James D. Matthews (March 1839 - June 1839 - Mounted Rangers) played a role in protecting the settlers in Northeast Texas.

Bowie County and Lamar County in northern Texas were both established by acts of the fifth Congress in Dec 1840. The County seat for Lamar County was originally the small settlement of Lafayette, located several miles northwest of the present County seat of Paris.

The exact expeditions of Captain Matthews's company are not all known. Pension papers, however show that a least one expedition was made of twelve days duration from Sep. 17-29-1841.

While daily operations of these three northern Texas ranger companies are not well documented, their presence was certainly a comfort to the Red River area settlers who had long suffered random depredations.

A partial roster of Capt. Matthew's Lamar County Minutemen included: Thomas Wade Box and his brother William Young Box.

1841 - Robert C "Climp" Greaves. Rev. Robert Greaves was born in the State of Mississippi, and came to Texas in the latter 1830's, and his first work, besides being a Methodist Circuit rider, was as a member of the Republic of Texas Rangers in 1841. He was stationed with a minute man unit at what is now Daingerfield, when the report came that a band of Comanche Indians had murdered an entire family near what is now called Mt. Vernon, when the company at once was sent out in pursuit of the savages.

Shortly after this (1842), Rev. Greaves married Sophronia Ann King and moved to within some three or four miles of Blackjack Grove, where he lived for some 15 years or more and then moved to Erath County, but after spending a few years there, moved back to Hopkins County. After returning to Hopkins County, he started the first Methodist church, which was later named, Rea's Chapel, after the first pastor there. (Rollins 2002)

He was an itinerant Methodist preacher and probably one of the organizers of the Methodist church in Branom in the 1840's.

It is said that most of the children of Rev., Greaves were born in this County even though he moved and lived in Erath County, near Stephenville for a short while. Upon returning, Rev. Greaves lived in this County the rest of his life and farmed and preached. He died 4 January 1882 and is buried in the Mt. Zion graveyard. The Greaves descendants married into the Renfro, McGee and Thomas family.

1842 - Capt. Merit Branom. Merit B. Branom is one of the best-known pioneers who settled Hopkins County (still Lamar County then) in the Emblem Community and had the Branom Community named after him. He was born in the State of Missouri about 1820 and moved to this County about 1839 or 1840. He was reported to be of Catholic faith and French ancestry, therefore, didn't join the Presbyterian church right away, but later became a member along with their children. The minutes reflect that he was elected Deacon on September 7, 1879 and the financial reports show him as a large financial supporter of the church.

A local resident was interviewed about the good old days, "Having been in this place (Black Jack Grove) for more than 40 years it was our great pleasure to be intimately acquainted with many men who had lived in the County almost from its beginning. Living in the extreme western portion of the County, very naturally our acquaintanceship covered mostly this section. However, we knew quite a few living east of Sulphur Springs."

He goes on to speak of Capt. Branom, "He was a man of over average ability, for while he never had the opportunity to obtain an education, he was, nevertheless, one of the best posted men we ever knew and was of Judicial mind. He was a man who not only did right himself, but he believed in making others do right. He was a terror to all evil doers and having the courage of a lion and almost the physical strength of a giant, what he might pursue was always given respectful consideration. He had spent four years in the Confederate Army and was a Democrat in politics. In early days in Texas, his home was the stopping place for Sam Houston, between whom a strong bond of sympathy and affection existed. His home was always open to a stranger, for which accommodation he would not accept one cent in repayment."

When Merit B Branom was born on February 14, 1820, in Point Pleasant, Missouri, his father, Michael, was 45 and his mother, Angelique, a French Canadian, was 26. Michael was a trapper, hunter, and farmer along the Mississippi River. He was living in New Madrid County by at least 1808.

He was living at Little Prairie, the center of the terrible earthquake of 1811. From the Smithsonian magazine, we get an account of its significance:

"At 2:15 a.m. on December 16, 1811, residents of the frontier town of New Madrid, in what is now Missouri, were jolted from their beds by a violent earthquake. The ground heaved and pitched, hurling furniture, snapping trees and destroying barns and homesteads. The shaking rang church bells in Charleston, South Carolina, and toppled chimneys as far as Cincinnati, Ohio.

"The screams of the affrighted inhabitants running to and fro, not knowing where to go, or what to do—the cries of the fowls and beasts of every species—the cracking of trees falling...formed a scene truly horrible," wrote one resident.

As people were starting to rebuild that winter, two more major quakes struck, on January 23 and February 7. Each New Madrid earthquake had a magnitude of 7.5 or greater, making them three of the most powerful in the continental United States and shaking an area ten times larger than that affected by the magnitude 7.8 San Francisco earthquake of 1906. (Rusch 2011)

Dunklin County history states Michael placed his wife on a horse and walked across the crevices at the time of the earthquake.

Reportedly, Merit came to Texas after his mother died, but was still living in Missouri in 1821, when it became a state.

One story has it that he followed the Finley family to Texas seeking the affections of his future wife. (Rollins 2002) Another version has it that after living in Texas a brief period, he married Elizabeth 'Ellen' Findley, a sister to Ed Finley. It was written in the family Bible that he reportedly went back to Missouri to his old home and make her his wife, bringing her to Texas.

In either case, they married on November 27, 1842, in Lamar County, Texas and shows them residing there. The 1872 map of Hopkins County, shows he owned land just south of Sulphur River of what would be now called, Cooper Lake. They had 14 children in 20 years. Later, they moved to Pecan Grove settlement on land between Mt. Zion and Cumby and lived there their remaining years. He died on January 24, 1900, in Cumby, Texas, having lived a long life of 79 years, and was buried in the local cemetery there.

His son, William J. 'Bill' Branom was sheriff of Hopkins County for 6 years.

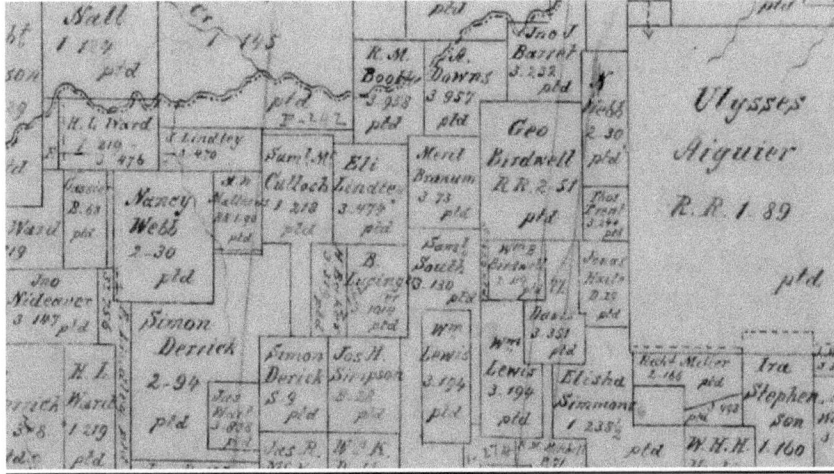

<u>1843 - Johnson Wren</u>. On the 1850 Census, he reported being born in Illinois and farming about 2000 acres. He also reported his sons being born in Texas which would make them living there about 1843. In that census, he was living and farming on land adjunct to <u>Curtis Jordan</u> and <u>Michael Garoutte</u>[10].

From the map, we know he owned two tracts of land in Branom Community, adjoining Halbrook and Cannon on the south of them. That is probably where the Herman brothers live, Benny and Rod, who have houses next to each other north of Hwy. 11 W. The road entry to their houses says, "Wren Creek Ranch."

---

[10] (Pronounced guh-ROOT)

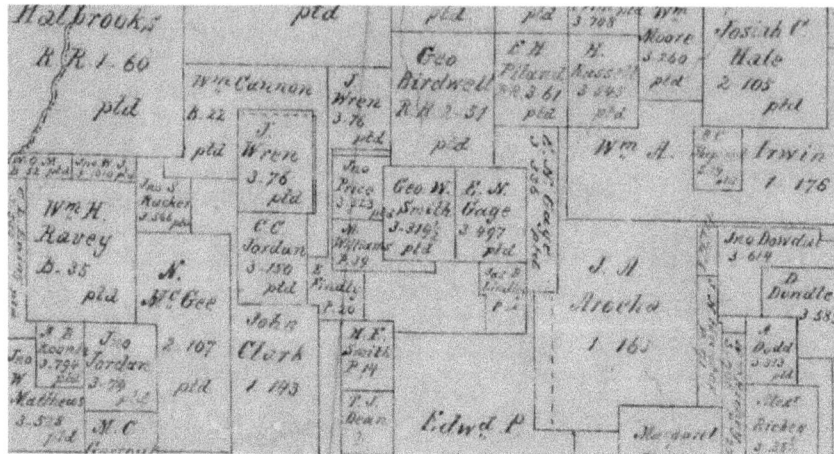

There is also a Wren cemetery, located just down the hill east of the Mt. Zion cemetery on the west side of Wren Creek. Reportedly, this was a rather large cemetery which was washed away by flooding in the past. (Rollins 2002)

In 1851, D. W. Cole purchased a tract of land that included the Black Jack grove from Elizabeth Wren, Johnson Wren's wife, and he began selling town lots.

In November 1853, Wren served in the 5th Legislature, sworn in 11/14/1853 as Senator elect from District No. 2, composed the counties of Lamar and Hopkins, presented his credentials, was qualified and took his seat.

In 1860, the Census reports him living with his family next to David Finley, Nicholas Harlow, and Finis Burns.

Wren died on 21 Nov 1862 and not much else is known about him.

Texas becomes a state

Looking at Texas from the perspective of the United States,

we can see three stages of frontier development evolving: first, establishing trade, then, settlement and, finally, *statehood*. When the United States accepted Texas into the union, Mexico still had not recognized Texas as an independent republic. Therefore, tensions increased between Mexico and the United States. Texas also had some difficulties making the transition from an independent republic to a state under a different form of government. However, this did not slow down the migration to Texas.

As the result of these tensions, a war erupted between the United States and Mexico that last about two years when the fighting ended in September 1847 when the U. S. Army captured Mexico City. About 8018 Texans volunteered to fight in this conflict sending more men to this conflict than any other state. With this victory, the western boundary of Texas, the Rio Grande, was settled.

About <u>1844 - John F. Taliaferro</u> – Records first show him in Texas when he married <u>Emily C. BABB</u> from Alabama and they had their first child by 1845. The Taliaferro family were prominent people who originally settled in Maryland and Virginia. At this point, not much else is known about him, especially when and where he died. Nevertheless, we know she remarried into the Garoutte family later in the Branom Community and had several additional children. Her daughter, Texanna Taliaferro, married into the Alexander family.

<u>1845 - Emily C. Babb</u> was married twice and not much is known about her family of origin, except that they came from Alabama, as did <u>Jemima Babb</u>, who married into the Box family.

<u>1846 – Alexander M. Ritchey</u>. He first appears on the records as a

landowner in Lamar County. From Ancestry.com we learned that Alexander's land patent in Texas was situated on the north side of the waters of White Oak Creek about 8 miles northwest of Sulphur Springs, according to the deed records. The land was near the area of Gafford's Chapel Cemetery, which makes it in present day, Hopkins County[11]. It appears they lived in Kentucky before migrating to Texas.

His daughter, Mary Elizabeth, was married to more than one pioneer of this Community: Curtis C. Jordan who died after she had 2 daughters with him, then William M. Cameron, who she married in her mid-twenties and had several other children. He was from Canada and was about 37, having only been in the United States about 3 years.

1846 – Rev. James Young – He was an early Methodist minister in the Hopkins County area from Tennessee where he fought in the War of 1812. His son, Fletcher Young, was also a Methodist preacher, who fought in the Civil War.

According to R.W. Harris, he (Fletcher Young) was a well-known preacher and universally beloved man, who lived down in the Gafford's Chapel Community. He would divide his last dollar with the poor unfortunate who would apply to him for aid and it was often said of the man that contributions given him as means of support he would often give away to others whom he thought needed the help worse than he. He also belonged to Co. K, 9th Texas Cavalry and fought under Gen. Sul Ross. The writer never heard any one speak one word of disapprobation of Rev. Young, but all who knew him venerated and esteemed him. He is buried

---

[11] source: Jeanne Branom.

in Oakland graveyard, there to wait the Resurrection morn. (Tuck 1932)

1847 - Michael C. Garoutte – He first shows up in Hopkins County when he married Emily C. BABB as her second husband. He was from New Jersey and of French origin (two generations up). Consequently, his sympathy leaned more for the union than confederates when the war broke out. Additionally, he must have had some degree of wealth because he bought land from the Halbrock and Rucker family. They also established their own small family cemetery, which is referenced elsewhere.

1848-1850 – Jessie C. Garrett – He moved to Texas in 1848 and to Hopkins County in 1850 with his family from Tennessee. On one occasion, he came to Black Jack Grove from the Miller Grove area where they settled and joined a command under Captain Merit Branom on an expedition against the Indians who had recently committed some depredations only a few miles to the northwest. They succeeded in dispersing the Indians, killing several of them and driving the remainder to the far West. He also fought with Branom in Company K during the Civil War, participating in many battles. He also served as a County commissioner for the Miller Grove precinct.

1848 – Rev. Laird (Lard) Burns. He seems to have moved to Texas from Missouri and has been discussed in more detail elsewhere.

1849 – Rev. Anthony Travelstead. He was a Cumberland Presbyterian preacher who lived in Lamar County, Paris and traveled to outlying areas. He helped establish the Presbyterian church in the Branom Community and is discussed in more detail elsewhere.

1850 – John B. S. Ewing (or McEwing). We first see him and his family on the 1850 Census living in Hopkins County. He is related to the Finis Ewing family and his wife was a <u>MILLS</u>. The family was closely associated with the Cumberland Presbyterian church and were found in Red River County early on. They lived in Kentucky, Missouri, and Arkansas before moving to Texas. His son, George S. Ewing, was 23 when they were listed on that census and he is listed as a landowner on the 1872 map. He married Nancy Caroline MATTHEWS, from the early pioneer family.

Hopkins County was formally established as a County of Texas in March of 1846 in the northeastern region of the state. The district, named for pioneer <u>David Hopkins</u> and his family of Indiana, was initially comprised of portions of Lamar and Nacogdoches Counties. Created at the geographic center of the County, as required by law at the time, the town of Tarrant was the original County seat. (Fullmore c1915) It is considered that David Hopkins and his family settled in Lamar County in 1840, where his parents died. In the winter of 1843 or 1844, he moved what is to what is now Hopkins County and married Annie Hargrove in 1846. A.J. Hopkins, a family member, was elected the first County clerk and died that same year, according to Judge Fullmore, the author of that source.

Besides Judge Fillmore, other sources identify Frank (Francis) Hopkins of Kentucky as the earlier settler in the area (1823) and there are indications that this family were the original pioneers for whom Hopkins County was named. It's questionable if the two families are related (David Hopkins family). (Richardson c1940) (McCuistion 1995)

Francis Hopkins is listed as owning a major tract of land, suggesting a grant for settling in Texas early on.

One of Frank Hopkins family married James Clark, person for whom the city of Clarksville was named. Also, another of Frank Hopkins relatives married a niece of James Clark, Nancy Clark. Members of both families were involved in political affairs in the decisions made when Hopkins County was created. Several are named in the story below. Records indicate that J.E. Hopkins and Eldridge Hopkins were different people, with the later probably called, 'Ell.'

The location of the original County courthouse was suggested by a committee made up of James E. Hopkins, Robert Hargrave, James Ward, William Wilkins and a man named Barker. They were charged to find the center of the County and to select two places within three miles of the center and to order an election to determine which of the two should be the location of the County seat which should be called Tarrant. The act does not so state, but this name was given in honor of General Edward Tarrant of Bowie County (at the time) who had done such valiant service in defending the settlers from the Indians. They determined the center by actual survey, and of both Hopkins family members offered to donate the land for the County seat. An election was held in which 110 votes were cast with Eldredge Hopkins' proposition winning by a vote of 50 to 60. This location was on the high prairie just north of where Rawson's store once stood - the Sulphur Springs and Birthright road passing through the location of the old town. The land was mostly owned by Shed Sickles and Mrs. John Chester. A town was laid off, lots were sold, stores were built, a court house and jail were erected by 1853, and Tarrant became quite a thriving village. Eldredge Hopkins built a hotel and was the town's most prominent citizen. It has always been claimed that it was for him that the County was named, but some of the early settlers dispute this, claiming that it was named for the Hopkins family and not for Eldredge Hopkins individually. (McDonald 1928)

From the Hopkins County Genealogical website, we have the following story:

In the year of 1848 Frank Pierce was a member of the Grand Jury, during the sitting of the District Court at old Tarrant, John T. Mills presiding judge.

The courthouse was built of logs and the Grand jury occupied a small log cabin which was built of poles upon the banks of a little dry branch some three hundred yards east from the court house building. Eldridge Hopkins, who was County clerk, ran a boarding house; this house consisted of a couple of log cabins with hall and piazza on either side. The Grand jury, the judge and attorneys boarded with Mr. Hopkins during the sitting of the court.

The Grand jury was composed of Harry Hargrave, Frank Pierce,

Carroll Crisp, Joe Salmon, Harry Hopkins, the names of the other members of this body have passed from the mind of Mr. Pierce. The planks that were placed upon the sleepers of Mr. Hopkins cabin hotel were not confined by nails. He accommodated all the court and some of their wives to lodging, and was a jolly good fellow. The judge convened court on Monday and dismissed it on the following Saturday at twelve o'clock. There were no convictions, no bills of indictment found. When the jury was discharged and court adjourned, the jury was paid for their services in County script, which Mr. Hopkins accepted in payment for board.

Only one incident transpired during the sitting of this court that is worthy of record. Col. Bill Young, prosecuting attorney, and Brad Fowler indulged too freely during the week and got on a high lonesome[12]. They, too, boarded at Eldridge Hopkins hotel. When these two gentlemen became too gay and hilarious, Mr. Hopkins in a persuasive and kindly manner asked them to respect his guests. One night in the week Col. Young secured a pair of Texas cowboy spurs, these spurs were profusely and lavishly belled. He arranged with Brad Fowler that he place himself in the position of a horse, and he would ride him over the hotel floor. This feat was performed in the still hours of the night. When Fowler began to pitch, in imitation of a mustang horse, the bells upon the spurs began to tinkle, the loose plank in the floor began to rattle, and Young hallowing " Woah, woah, woah," a noise fell upon the ears of the inmates like the crack of doom and frightened them, men and women, almost senseless. It appeared to the inmates of the hotel that his satanic majesty with all of his imps had come upon them with the fury of a tornado and that destruction and

[12] *Gloomy and bleak*

devastation was upon them. Men and women left their beds and pallets and sought safety in the open air. When the excitement and alarm was over and it was ascertained that the trick was all a joke, the guests returned to their sleeping quarters and rested till day. This incident was a subject of talk for months after.

There was one whiskey house in the village of Tarrant, owned and run by Tom Louden, tin cups were used for glasses, and gourds for dippers. When court adjourned each juryman bought a Spanish gourd of whiskey, hung the gourd by means of a raw hide string tied around its center to the horn of the saddle, and [carried] himself to his home. The refined and delicate feeling of the reader, may be shocked at the foregoing incident. This is an occurrence of real life, and the actors of this scene have long since passed from the stage of life, gone to learn the dread reality of an unknown world. When God lays his hands upon a man the world should let him rest. No more will we hear of the actions of these men until we all meet on eternity's wave, beyond death's chilling flood, to enjoy the association of the angels of heaven in eternity. (www.accessgenealogy.com 2012)

Founded in the latter part of the 1840's, the city of Bright Star was a haven for the early settlers with more than 100 natural springs rising up from the ground. Later, the County seat was moved and renamed, Sulphur Springs.

When Hopkins County was organized, the entire state of Texas was probably less than 100,000, and Hopkins County had a very scattered population estimated to be 500 to 600 people in the County. Not much taxes could be collected, consequently there were no funds with which to build a courthouse. It seems that at that time there was an old law on the statute books forbidding outsiders to being cattle into the state for grazing purposes, but one Pleasants or Pleasance from Louisiana, disregarding this law, drove three hundred head to pasture on the prairies of Hopkins County. These cattle were confiscated and sold, and a courthouse and jail were erected at Tarrant with the proceeds. The courthouse was a frame building and the jail was built of hewed logs.

When they had a particularly bad prisoner or one that was likely to be rescued by his friends, they took him to Clarksville where they had a brick jail.

Because of the scattered population, it was easier for individuals to stand out if they made a significant contribution to the area.

1849 – <u>David M. Finley</u> – Before he moved from Missouri, David M Finley married Margaret McIwaine in 1836 when he was 21 years old. He was a charter member of the Harmony Presbyterian Church in Mt. Zion, Hopkins County, Texas (1 of 13 members along with his wife, Margaret, brother & sister-in-law, also a Deacon). Served as tax assessor for Hopkins County and nephew of Ellen Findley Branom.

They were probably of Scottish origin.

1849 – <u>Lewis Finley</u> – Younger brother of David M Finley. Was a charter member of the Harmony Presbyterian Church in Mt. Zion, Hopkins County, Texas (1 of 13 members along with his wife, brother & sister-in-law). Lewis' oldest child was Edmund born in Texas (referred to as Ed-III).

Harmony Presbyterian established at Mt Zion

1849-1850: The Cumberland Presbyterian at Mt Zion, was organized in 1849 by Rev. Anthony Travelstead with 13 members.

Many of the early settlers in Lamar County and surrounding areas were from Kentucky, Tennessee, and Missouri and of Scots-Irish descent, therefore, had Presbyterian roots. The minutes of the church lists those 13 charter members as:

MALES	FEMALES
Ezekial Campbell	Lottie Campbell
Louis Finley	Lettie Finley
*David Finley	Margaret Finley
*John S Rucker	Mary Rucker
Adolphus Harlow	Almira Harlow
*F. Marrs	Julia Marrs
*Deacons ordained in 1850	Ellen Branom
	(Butler) 1967)

We pause for a moment to account for each member who we know lived there at this time.

Ezekial Campbell	Lottie Campbell

They were both from Tennessee, were married and had their first child in Arkansas and the rest of them there, then moved to Texas by 1849 when they showed up on the church rolls. They lived in Hopkins County for the next 20 years, then we lose track of them after 1860.

It is unclear if they were related to Crockett H. Campbell, who was born in 1816, and came to Hopkins County in the year 1841. There was not a single cabin on the south side of North Sulphur Creek at that time. Buffalo herds were roaming all over the country. He had shot and killed many buffalo as well as all kinds of animals and wild beasts. Indians were to be seen and heard in many places, and a few people who were living in tents were in constant and perpetual dread of them. Many emigrants who came into the new country, became dissatisfied, alarmed, and returned to their old homes in the States.

In the year 1843 Campbell married Elizabeth Collins. By this union eight children were born, four of whom are living. He had the misfortune to lose his wife, and subsequently married Miss Mary Couch. They were the parents of eight children, six boys and two girls. Crockett Campbell farmed and raised stock all his life. He was a man of noble qualities. His example has been good. He is beloved by all who knew him." (www.accessgenealogy.com 2012)

Louis (Lewis) Finley	Lettie Finley
*David-II Finley	Margaret Finley

These two brothers and their families have already been discussed as their father was a pathfinder in this area.

*John Sherman Rucker	Mary Rucker

John S and Mary HARLOW Rucker were early landowners in this area, owning property near the South Sulphur river. He was from Cooper County, Missouri where they were married in 1845, before moving to Texas. They were in their early 20's when they joined the church and moved to Denton/Grayson County area after the Civil War where they died.

Adolphus Harlow   Almira Harlow

It looks like Adolphus and Almira were Mary Rucker's siblings who joined the church with them since they were younger and married later after this event. They moved on to live in other parts of Texas.

The Koontz family also married into the Harlow family and settled in the area about the same time.

For example, Andrew Brown Koontz was born May 16, 1827, in Nicholas Co., [West] Virginia, son of Alexander Koontz and Susan Martin. Andrew was married April 28, 1847, to Martha Jane Harlow, who was born about 1827 in Virginia, probably Albemarle County, daughter of Nicholas Harlow and Jeanetta Bridgwater. The marriage was performed by Rev. John F. Clark at the Heath Creek Baptist Church in Cooper Co., Missouri, where many Mt. Zion residents moved from.

Andrew and Martha Koontz were living in Hopkins Co., Texas, by 1850. They moved there not long after the birth of their first child. Andrew was primarily engaged in farming the 160 acres he received by patent from the Texas government in 1857. Andy and Mattie, as they were called, remained in Hopkins County for many years and raised a large family. Andy was farming successfully but, like so many, his progress was affected by the Civil War. The value of his personal and real property in 1860 was $5,100, a fair sum for the times. After the war and by the next census in 1870, his estate was valued at $3,900.

Andrew suffered from bronchitis the last two years of his life. He died May 14, 1912, in Wood Co., Texas, and was buried the following day near his homestead.

Their daughter, Sarah Jane Koontz first married 1) John F. Wilkinson, and then, 2) <u>Samuel Ely (Eli) Miller</u>, from another pioneer family. She is buried in the Mt. Zion cemetery, along with several other Millers. Samuel served in the 1st Cav in Mississippi and apparently moved to Texas after the Civil War like many who did during that period.

Of special interest from this family, we have a concrete tomb located above ground in the Mt. Zion cemetery that seldom goes unnoticed but has little documentation. Below is the best explanation found so far:

"Tale told to me as a child. That the vault was left by the side of the road. My Grandmother was Zena Connor and her parents were John Connor and Lillie Mae Koontz. John Connor and Lillie Mae Koontz were Buried in Perryville at the Perryville Cemetery. John Calhoun Connor/Conner has a very nice tombstone, but Lillie Mae's tombstone is missing. I do have relatives buried in Mt. Zion Cemetery. I believe that Martha Jane Harlow Koontz may be buried in the tomb that has only Koontz on it." (Cunningham 2016)

No other explanation has been offered and that concrete tomb is currently association with Martha Jane HARLOW Koontz's grave.

*F. Marrs   Julia Marrs

There was a Marrs family living in Red River County whose daughter, Rachel Marrs, had married Jesse Shelton. They lived in Miller County, Arkansas and, later, the Roxton/Paris area. They seem to all have moved from Missouri and some may have moved <u>back</u> to Missouri after the Civil War.

Franklin and Juliana, the Marrs family who were early

members of the Mt. Zion Presbyterian Church, were first recorded in Texas in 1849 and later (1855 & 1859) when he bought land in the area. It appears they stayed in Hopkins County and were buried in the Cumby Cemetery.

Ellen FINLEY Branom, the final charter member, had been in Texas the longest and her history ties in with her husband, Capt. M. Branom, whose pioneer history has already been discussed and the Ed Finley family.

A.J. McGown, an early circuit preacher for the Cumberland Presbyterian Church in Texas, was an early advocate for recruiting both ministers and families to move from the states to Texas. In the spring of 1844, he embarked on a one-man ministerial recruitment crusade for the church in Texas. For nearly a year, he pursued his goal as he traveled through Louisiana, Alabama, Mississippi, Tennessee and Kentucky saturating the countryside with information about Texas and its religious needs. (Brackenridge 1968)

In 1846 or 1847, Israel Folsom, **my 3rd great-uncle** and husband of 3rd great-aunt, wrote a letter to the Red River Presbytery requesting that a minister be sent to the Choctaw Nation in what is now Oklahoma. The result was that Folsom, Samuel McKee, and Benjamin Spencer were licensed to preach and teach to the Choctaw Nation missions, hold revivals, and establish churches with the support of the Presbytery in Red River. (Brackenridge 1968)

Pastors who served in the Presbyterian Church:

1849 - Anthony Travelstead. He lived in the Paris area where a Presbyterian presence had been established as early as 1843 and preached over a wide area, including Clarksville, in Red River

County, Charleston, in what is now Delta County, taking donations or, at times, nothing, when he wasn't making a living as a carpenter.

Known locally as 'grandpa' Travelstead, he lived on two acres of land bought from George Wright, an early settler, just outside corporate city limits of Paris. It adjoined two acres that Wright had sold to Francis Miles, part of which is now covered by the brick houses on Deep Bonham street. He opened a street between the two tracts and, for a time it was called Travelstead street.

He was known for his piety, humor and eloquence...and loud voice, which was heard by many people when he engaged in prayer. Once a young man in Clarksville said to him, "Mr. Travelstead, why so you pray so loud? Do you think the Lord is deaf?" Grandpa looked at the youth for a moment and said, "No son, I don't think the Almighty is deaf, but I know he is such a long way from this ungodly place." The conversation ended there.

<u>1848 – Laird (Lard) Burns</u>. Laird, who later used the name (Lard), Jr. BURNS was born in 1784 in Chester County, Camden District, South Carolina. His ancestors were Americans who were descendants of Presbyterian and other Ulster Protestant Dissenters from various parts of Ireland, even though they were originally from Scotland.

He was the son of Laird BURNS, Sr. and Jennett BURNS, Also, the great grandson of John B. Burns, a farmer and blacksmith, who some say made the first cannon used in the Revolutionary War. Their roots trace back all the way to Scotland and the surname went through different spellings, like Bourns, ...

He has the distinction of being one of the earliest people

buried in the Mt Zion Cemetery (January 1858, the same year land was donated for the church and cemetery that December). The location is Section SW, Row 4, gravesite 11.

His first marriage was to Jean Williams in Mecklenburg, North Carolina on January 30, 1801, when he was 17 years old. She died approximately 10 years later, cause of death unknown. Nothing is currently known about children.

He is buried next to his second wife, Mary Polly WEIR (WEAR). They wed 2 Jan 1812 in Russellville, Logan County, Kentucky. She was born in 1792 in North Carolina, the daughter of Hugh WEIR and Margaret LYLE. Mary died in 1861 in Hopkins County. They had at least 8 children, who lived to adulthood.

Thanks to church records, we know he became a candidate for the ministry in the Cumberland Presbyterian Church in Missouri 12 Sep 1820; was licensed 12 Sep 1821; and ordained 5 Apr 1833. This was during the early days of formation of the Cumberland Presbyterian Church. Records show that on February 4, 1810, at the home of Rev. Samuel McAdow near present day Dickson, Tennessee, McAdow, Rev. Finis Ewing, and Rev. Samuel King reorganized Cumberland Presbytery, previously dissolved by Kentucky Synod of the Presbyterian Church (USA). Laird was an early colleague who studied under these men in Missouri and did missionary work at camp meetings.

The reader will note that Rev. Burns was greatly influenced by these three men and vice versa. Laird named one of his sons after Finis Ewing and Ewing's relatives ended up living in Hopkins County during the early days (George S. Ewing). The Ewings also intermarried with the Mills family more than once.

Psychologically, we know this about him. When admitted as a

member of the presbytery, he was approved to have an experimental knowledge of religion, felt a call to the ministry, had several men provide testimonials of his moral character. After leaving Missouri, a Judge Ewing (one of Finis Ewing's relatives who ended up living in Texas and working at Trinity University) reminisced: "Laird Burns was also one of the early ministers of the neighborhood. He was a man of respectable abilities ... He was very amiable in his intercourse with men, and upright in his Christian character. "

Although strange to us today, he also owned slaves. In the 1830 census, it was reported he had 15 slaves in Cooper County, Missouri. When Lard died he only had one slave (Malinda), valued at $50. He died before the Civil War, but at least 4 of his sons served, probably for the Confederacy. John Perry served for the South.

Prior to the Civil War, the state of Missouri and its citizens owned less than 10% slaves, so it was not heavily invested in the economic benefits of slavery.

At some point in time, Rev. Finis Ewing took a stand against slavery. As early as 1835, he published a sermon in which he took strong ground against at least some of the evils of slavery. Prior to that, the Cumberland Presbyterian Church was considered a slave-holding Church, with great freedom, and members owned slaves until after the Civil War.

In the progress of the sermon he (Rev. Ewing) gives the following as his own experience and purposes in relation to his slaves: "Lest some of my readers," says he, "should say, 'Physician, heal thyself,' I think it proper to state in this place, that after a long, painful, and prayerful investigation of the subject, I have determined. not to hold, nor to give, nor to sell, nor to buy any slave for life, mainly from the influence of that passage of God's word which says, 'Masters, give unto your servants that which is just and equal.'" The result of his experience and resolution was, that at his death all his servants were emancipated. (Beard 1867)

Lard and Mary had four sons in the Confederate Army (denoted with *). Spouses are also listed:

- James M. Burns (born in KY) married Margaret FORSYTHE

- *Hugh B. W. Burns, Rev. (born in KY) married Martha Ann WARREN

- John Perry W. B. Burns (born in Ala) married Lucenda Jane BURKE in Missouri and came with him to Texas, first to Titus County (before it became Morris County in 1875), then Hopkins County (buried in Mt Zion). Her father, Lindsey B. Burke, also eventually moved to Hopkins County by the mid-1850's.

- *Finis Ewing Burns (born in MO) married Julia BROWN

- Margaret "Mattie" Burns (born in MO) married William STEWART

- *Samuel Jackson Burns (born in MO) married Elizabeth BURKE (buried in Mt Zion)

- *George B. Burns (born in MO)

- Mary Francis Burns (born in MO) married James W. CLARK

The reader familiar with the Branom Community will begin to recognize Mt Zion families who married into the Burns ancestors:

Burke, Stewart, etc. Many other families married ancestors of Laird Burns, Jr. For example, my own family, my dad's mothers' people, a Raines, married a Burns. My mother's dad's sister, a Pipkin, married a Burns. Technically, he was the **paternal grandfather and husband of my great-aunt.**

This pattern of inter-marrying results in people often referring to ancestors of this Community at the 'Mt Zion family' and it probably was dysfunctional as most other families are, including church families in all denominations.

Laird died 28 Jan 1858 in Hopkins Co., Texas, and was buried in Mt Zion Cemetery shortly thereafter. Reportedly, he carried the name "Laird" until he moved to Texas when he dropped the "i" and spelled it "Lard."

Sons John Perry and Hugh Wear Burns both became preachers for the Cumberland Presbyterian Church, helping establish a church in Miller Grove, Texas, the southern end of Hopkins County.

Laird left New Lebanon Presbytery 9 Oct 1848, possibly for retirement, even though his regular job was farming, and moved to Texas shortly thereafter. He was in his mid-60's at this time. It is <u>not</u> known that he served as pastor at Mt. Zion, but he most certainly would have been invited to preach.

<u>1848 - George Dawson Winnifred</u>. From Kentucky, he moved his family to Texas sometime around 1848 where we found one of his daughters married in Ellis County. In March 1860, he married Sarah A. "Ann" ALEXANDER. In 1862, he enlisted in Company K, Texas 30th Cavalry Regiment and survived the war. His descendants lived around Cumby and gradually moved to Commerce, Greenville, Dallas and the northeast Texas area to

work. The Wiggs family also married into the Winnifred family. One of his descendants, James R. Winniford, taught this writer biology in high school in Commerce, Texas and was a Church of Christ preacher for many years.

Summary

By the end of this period, we can see how the Branom Community was influenced by people who came from Missouri to settle. Many were not only people of faith, but specifically Cumberland Presbyterians and of Scots-Irish descent. When Texas became a state, it experienced the most rapid growth in its history. As a border state, they were less likely to support slave ownership and, as working-class farmers, they were less likely to own their land.

Historically, people of faith were persecuted by unlawful settlers and they had to move from one place to another until they settled in where they were better received. The customs were different, according to the specific denomination. The Mormons are an extreme example of this situation because they practiced polygamy. They had to rely on the following qualities, as all people of faith must, to survive:

- Faith: With faith the pioneers followed their leaders or convictions and endured persecutions.

- Determination: They were determined to live the gospel and to overcome their personal trials.

- Dedication: They fulfilled their responsibilities and duties.

- Patience: They were willing to be patient because they could see the vision, they had a glimpse of what they could have.

- Endurance: They endured whatever persecutions they had. To endure is to not only endure the hardships in this life but also to do it while preparing for eternity.

- Good work ethic: The pioneers were responsible. They saw a job to completion.

- Priority driven: They aligned priorities with needs versus their wants. Surviving forced this on people; otherwise, they met an untimely death.

- Cooperation and respect: They had cooperation and respect for others.

People with little to no faith, like the Comanches and lawless settlers, and people of grossly different faith and beliefs, like fundamentalists, were outright hostile to people of faith who were sincere, especially early pioneers who were more visible in the Community.

Thus, many pioneers ended up trusting in the reality of things that are still "invisible" and secret. It kept them on the search. This was the essence of faith, whereas what many people who settle want is perfect certitude and clarity before every step forward. Certainty and clarity does not sustain great or strong people.

Appearing in this period are descendants of pathfinder families who stayed, settled, and served:

Lewis and Lettie Finley family.

David-II and Margaret Finley family.

Ellen FINLEY Branom family.

The following appear for the first time in the area during this period (1831 to 1850) and began serving the Community:

About 1830 - Edward H. Tarrant family.

1834 – Thomas Avis Yates, Jr. family.

1835 – Joseph Cromwell Matthews family.

1835 – Curtis C. Jordan family.

1836-37 – M.M. Green family.

1837 – Jesse Shelton family.

1837 – Henry McDonald family.

1837 – James Frances Box family.

1842 - Robert C Greaves family.

1842 - Capt. Merit Branom family.

1843 – John Wren family.

1844 – John Taliaferro family.

1845 – Babb family.

1846 – DeSpain family.

1846 – Ritchey family.

1846 – Rev. James Young family.

1847 - Michael C. Garoutte family.

1848 - George Dawson Winnifred. & Sarah A. "Ann" ALEXANDER.

In addition to the above, from the Presbyterian church records, we know the following were living in the area by <u>1849</u>:

Ezekial and Lottie <u>Campbell</u> family.

John S. and Mary <u>HARLOW Rucker</u> family.

Adolphus and Almira <u>Harlow</u> family.

The <u>Koontz family.</u>

Franklin and Julia <u>Marrs</u> family.

Pastors who served in the Presbyterian Church:

<u>1849 - Anthony Travelstead</u> family.

<u>1848 – Laird (Lard) Burns</u> family.

<u>1848-50 – Jessie Garrett</u> family.

<u>1849 – F. Marrs and Julia Marrs</u> family.

<u>1849 – Lindley</u> family.

<u>1850 – John Ewing</u> family.

Additional families that were living in and around Hopkins County who helped pioneer the way for those who followed are:

Bingham family

Curlee family

Taylor family

Plunkett family – several family members buried at the Plunket-Pleasant Grove cemetery

O.D. and Ollie Gillis family – several family members buried at the Plunket-Pleasant Grove cemetery

Cate family

To the growing list of scots-Irish backgrounds, we add at least two pioneers with French ancestry, the Branom and Garoutte families. These families interacted with each other, attending social events, schools, churches, and intermarrying. For example, their descendants, like the Branom family, intermarried with the Camerons, Ritcheys, Garouttes, and Butlers. There was a nucleus of families from Cooper County, Missouri who moved into the Branom Community that had pre-existing relationships: the Ewing, Finley, Wear (Weir), Burns and Branom families.

Though not all-inclusive, we know there were over 30 families who were living in Hopkins County during this time and are referred to as 'pioneer families'.

3 PIONEERS: STAGES OF SETTLEMENT

On a personal, family level, settling in on the frontier involved securing housing. This would involve moving from tent living to a more solid structure, like a cabin or house. Nearby water and fertile soil would be as important as safety from native attacks and criminal acts. If religious, like family-oriented settlers were, the need for religious services would eventually surface, such as marrying, worshipping, baptizing and burying.

The mainstream Presbyterians and Congregationalists, since they depended on well-educated ministers, were shorthanded in evangelizing the frontier. Most frontiersmen showed little commitment to religion until traveling evangelists began to appear and to produce "revivals". The local pioneers responded enthusiastically to these events, which featured outdoor camp meetings lasting a week or more and which introduced many people to organized religion for the first time.

The Baptists set up small independent churches, founded on the principle of independence of the local congregation. On the other hand, bishops of the well-organized, centralized Methodists assigned circuit riders to specific areas for several years at a time, then moved them to fresh territory. Several new denominations were formed, of which the largest was the Disciples of Christ, somewhat related doctrinally to the Church of Christ and Presbyterians.

Camp Meetings

First, they started with camp meetings. These were an outgrowth of the circuit rider system of the Methodist and

Cumberland Presbyterian Churches, both being invested in having camp meetings on the frontier. Emotionalism played a significant role in the services, especially the camp-meeting revivals. Men cried, women fainted, young people became hysterical. 'They call it a revival' wrote one critical observer. (Campbell 2003)

Probably the earliest and most accurate account of the origin of camp meetings comes from the unpublished booklet gathered by Mrs. A.S. Broadfoot. She quotes a local resident, Joe Young, grandson of the 1846 Methodist minister, James Young, who claimed to know when and where the meetings began. As the story goes, they began with Methodist camp meetings when the circuit riders would come around before Texas became a state or Hopkins County became a County or churches in that area had land or buildings. This would have been in the early 1840's. The church meetings were held in homes, under arbors and in school houses and they became known as Camp Meetings.

Later, the exact spot in the Branom Community was located down a present dirt road, just north of the Mt Zion church, at a place once called, 'Birchy Bluff.' When the Cotton Belt railroad ran a line through the County in 1884, they made a switch track at Birchy Bluff and called it 'Dunsmore Switch.' (A.S. Broadfoot 1967)

Young said people prepared the year 'round for those annual meetings, curing meat, drying fruit, grinding wheat and corn for bread, making kraut, hominy, brought live chickens, and even cows for milk. They brought Dutch ovens and big iron wash pots for heating water, cleaning utensils and, even, washing clothes for large families. Eventually, during the two-week encampment, stews were cooked in the large pots and became known as, 'Hopkins County Stew.'

From the historical files of June E. Tuck (who does not validate or dispute any historical facts in the article), we learn that, over time, these were as much reunions as religious services. They were really devoted to what the word implies, a reuniting of old timers. It was a distance out in the country, and people came in wagons and other conveyances and were prepared to camp out in a real old settler manner, under the shade of the trees, seated on logs and stumps, with likely a few old fashioned, split bottom chairs available, these old veterans of an early day renewed the associations of the frontier times, smoked and talked.

Occasionally someone, oratorically inclined, would enliven the proceedings with interesting anecdotes and, in all probability, old time singing was indulged in. The younger element would withdraw a safe distance, and, unknown to Pa and Ma, would enjoy a reunion of their own, ... and they would assume new and more tender relations so far as this life was concerned. Several days were thus spent by old and young, in innocent enjoyment, with an expense that was negligible. (Tuck 1932)

As time passed and churches were established, variations of the local gatherings morphed into reunions, end-of-the-stews (which eventually were called, 'Hopkins County stews'), and revivals or 'protracted meetings'. A remnant of these gatherings still exists today at the Mt. Zion cemetery when they hold their annual reunion and gathering of the general membership (stockholders). The format includes a worship service with a program speaker, pot luck lunch, annual business meeting followed by a meeting of the board of trustees. Another remnant exists in the Community in what is known as a 'Lytle stew', which historically has been an annual gathering of men who cook stew (or chili or fry fish) and socialize from after lunch until the last one

77

leaves. It has been located on Lytle farmland and blends university personnel with local residents.

Brief History of area Churches

As life progressed through the settlement of the area, people met in homes until churches could be erected. Buildings were related to the religious preferences of people who settled the area and were often shared with other denominations when funding was scarce.

Brief History of the Cumberland Presbyterian Church. It was a result of the Great Revival of 1800. A disagreement surfaced over the mechanics of the revival and over allowances the pro-revival faction was willing to make in order to secure ministers for its rapidly expanding following.

In two presbyteries, Cumberland in particular, believed that that the revival to be an **extraordinary circumstance** which allowed for exceptions to both educational requirements for ordination and the required subscription to the Westminster Confession of Faith.

As the result, the Kentucky Synod, ruling body, dissolved Cumberland Presbytery.

On February 4, 1810, at the home of Rev. Samuel McAdow near present day Dickson, Tennessee, McAdow, Rev. Finis Ewing, and Rev. Samuel King reorganized Cumberland Presbytery, previously dissolved by Kentucky Synod of the Presbyterian Church (USA).

These disaffected Presbyterian ministers did not intend to found an independent Presbyterian body. They felt that they would have greater success resolving their differences with Kentucky Synod as an organized body than as individuals. They also felt that the organization of a presbytery would better enable them to serve their congregations.

Growing rapidly, Cumberland Presbytery became Cumberland Synod in 1813 and, in 1829, when a General Assembly was established, the Cumberland Presbyterian denomination was formed. Thus, two varieties of Presbyterian denominations were formed: the 'Old School' variety insisting on an educated ministry and the Cumberlands, who accepted uneducated ministers.

Cumberland Presbyterian (individual) congregations are governed by elected elders who make up a "session." Presbyteries are made up of ordained clergy and elder delegates from each congregation within their bounds. Presbyteries, in turn, send delegates to synods. Finally, the entire structure is governed by the General Assembly. The Assembly charges various boards and agencies with the day-to-day operation of the denomination.

Cumberland Presbyterian congregations are still located throughout the United States, but are primarily located in the American South.

The Cumberland Presbyterian denomination had a socially progressive tradition. Cumberland Presbyterians were among the first denominations to admit women to their educational institutions and to accept them in leadership roles including the ordained clergy.

Cumberland Presbyterian Church organized in Mt Zion. The first land was bought for the church January 3, 1882. The present building was erected in 1924.

Brief history of the Methodist Church in Texas and Mt. Zion

1815. The first ordained Methodist minister, and the first

Protestant minister, to preach in Texas was William Stevenson, a member of the Tennessee Conference who preached at Pecan Point in what is now Clarksville in Red River County during an exploratory journey in the fall of 1815. When Claiborne Wright's family moved to Pecan Point in 1816, they became the earliest Methodist family known in Texas. By the late 1830's, the Methodist circuit riders were actively working in Texas bringing 'Methodist excitement,' a highly emotional form of religion that propelled them to the number one denomination in Texas by 1860. (Campbell 2003)

<u>Mt Zion Methodist Episcopal Church</u>. This church was already in the Community, a working organized church, as noted in the minutes of the Greenville Circuit of the Methodist Church. The Methodist church had divided the country into sections or circuits and operated on the basis of circuit riders, preachers on horseback, who followed the migration to carry the gospel to settlers. Before churches could be built, worship was held in people's homes, school houses, and, primarily, in camp meetings. Thus, camp meetings and the circuit rider had a profound influence on extending the Methodist faith to the Southwest pioneers.

The Methodist Episcopal Church is to be distinguished from the Episcopal Church, which appealed to the planter/farmer elite and town dwellers and had relatively few members in Texas in the early days.

The first documented activity of Methodists working in the area was when <u>Robert C Greaves</u> and his wife, <u>Saphrona Ann KING</u>, came into the area in 1842. Their daughter, <u>LaVina 'Sis' GREAVES Burns </u>(Methodist), was married into the Lard Burns family, so there was a mixture of Presbyterians and Methodists

80

through marriage. LaVina is buried in Mt Zion in the Southeast section, row 2, space 7.

Other early pastors of the Methodist church were Joseph Proctor and James Young, along with his wife, Margaret. The building was erected in 1861 on land donated by David Finley and Nicolas Harlow. The alternated services and use of the building with the Presbyterians every two weeks.

In Commerce, two Methodist congregations, Lebanon (1.5 miles east) and Mt. Zion (5 miles southeast), served the earliest settlers of the Commerce area. (https://www.fumccommerce.org 2015)

Viola Hays Parsons published a booklet in 1939 and Mrs. P.B. Trawick in 1964 on the Commerce Methodist church that offers more information. Although physical copies of the booklets are unavailable, one source suggests that the first church was organized in 1843 and was known as Adeline's Chapel. This was located two miles south of town across the Athens Wagon Road (now Highway 11) from the home and farm of the late Mr. T. P. Hudson.

In 1914, the Methodist church moved east on Highway 11 and was named Rea's Chapel after the pastor. Other pastors associated with the Methodist church were Sam Blackburn, George Grace, John Hadbrock, William Kelly, Joseph Proctor, as well as James Young and Robert C. Greaves.

In Cumby, the Methodist Church charter members worshipped in an old school house that stood in what is now part of the Cumby Cemetery. Later, they worshipped with the Presbyterians. The deed for the property was executed June 25, 1892, and the First Methodist Church building was erected on

Frisco Street in 1894. The present building was erected in 1929.

Brief History of the Baptist Church

The organizational structure (locally administered vs. hierarchical) of the Baptist church makes it more difficult to pinpoint the beginnings in each Community.

In the Branom Community, it appears that the first Baptist church was organized on August 31, 1879 at a meeting on the old camp ground on the bank of the South Sulphur river. Family names recorded among the people present are: Lawson, Smith, Teer, Cumings, Farr, Rash, and Ladd. The actual records were handed down through the Vaughn family to Yvonne Rollins. (Rollins 2002)

Other records of the Baptist church in Mt. Zion go back to 1912 with notations suggesting a church was organized in 1885. Family names of members and church officers are: Vaughn, Neal, Boucher, Scott, Patrick, Smith, Evans, Jenkins and Tucker. In 1963, the Baptist church started sharing services in the Presbyterian church when Rea's Chapel Methodist church disbanded. (Rollins 2002)

Pastors associated with the Baptist church in Mt. Zion were: Roy Lee Dittmar, Paul Capehart, W.J. Humphrey, Ed Dickens, and Pastors Scudder, Allen, Short, Laven.

In Sulphur Springs, the Baptist church was organized in 1859. The Black Jack Grove Baptist Church had no other surviving records since theirs were burned. It was mentioned in the minutes of the Old Concord Baptist Church as it (Black Jack Grove Baptist) and another church, Twin Oaks put together a united advisory board in 1876 to sit and consider the dissolution of the

Old Concord church. In 1893, the church erected its first house of worship. The present First Baptist Church was built in 1943.

On a state level, the Baptist church stood second among denominations in 1860, only to the Methodists, then followed by the Cumberland Presbyterians. (Campbell 2003)

Schools

Few would remember that a lack of public education was one of the grievances listed toward the Mexican government in the Texas declaration of independence. It took joining the union before Texas could implement a public-school system, however, and the bill wasn't signed until 1854.

1850. Chapel Hill College. While the Cumberland Presbyterians were falsely labeled as light on 'book learning,' they did establish Chapel Hill College in Dangerfield, then Titus County prior to the organization of Morris County in 1875.

On January 8, 1849, Allen Urkhart gave land for the college on the condition it be built in Dangerfield. It was located on Highway 259 in Daingerfield near the Presbyterian Church. (T. H. Campbell 2017)

Urquhart gave forty (40) acres of land and pledged one half of the proceeds from the sale of his remaining lots in the original town Plat for the erection of the college buildings.

This male only college, Chapel Hill, operated from 1852 until 1869 when it was closed due to lack of students and finances. (McFarland 2010)

This event probably cemented the connection between this area and Cooper County, Missouri and brought additional families to the area. For example, John Wear (Weir), brother to Hugh Wear and ancestor of Catherine FINLEY Branom and Mary Polly WEAR (WEIR) Burns, served on the first board of trustees.

Pathfinders and pioneers had to rely on home schooling or private schooling if available. As people banded together in communities, little one-room schoolhouses sprang up. The number of teachers depended upon the size and make up of enrollment. It would be after the Civil War that public schools were designated.

Public Schools. In 1867, the Hopkins County Commissioners Court established 32 school districts. District No. 30 became known as Plunkett School in 1903 when a new schoolhouse was built at this site and named for its builder, James W. Plunkett (1829-1914). W. A. Smith, P. B. and Lizzie Wise, and O. D. and Ollie Gillis donated land for the school. The schoolhouse also served as a meeting place for two churches, the Cumberland Presbyterian Church and a non-denominational congregation. Due to declining enrollment, the school closed in 1945 and the building was razed.

Despite divisive issues about slavery creating conflicts in the Branom Community, they were able to pull together and consolidate efforts to provide education for their children. It is thought that the school at Branom opened as early as 1861.

Later, two preceding schools were merged: Greenwood and Pecan Schools. And, two additional schools joined, Willow Oak and Faulk Grove Schools, to make it a 4-teacher school. Grades 1-11 was as high as they went.[13] Thanks goes out to Yvonne Stewart Rollins for her contribution in helping preserve the history of this

---

[13] Rollins, 2001.

time and place.

Willow Oak was a one-room school where members of the Tucker family once attended.

Local history merges with local personalities here, as Dr. Warren T. Binion, a country physician who provided health care for that region after he obtained his medical license in 1889, taught school at the Pecan School. The Pecan School was east of where the Branom School was located toward Oakland Community.

The other was a one-room school in Greenwood, a Community of about 250 people three miles east of Commerce (and west of the Branom area) where Sam Rayburn previously taught school.

Families who contributed students to the Greenwood school in the 1906-1907 school year were: Stewart, Smith, Boucher, Burnes, Vaughn, Ladd, Patrick, Hammock, Garrett, Roan, Whitson, Bulls, and Brown.

Families who contributed students to the Pecan school were not listed, but from Rollins' work, we know they probably were living in the east end of the Branom Community toward Ridgeway: such as Broiles/Broyles, Finley, Binion, Branom, Green, Deakins, Butler, and Ross families. When consolidated, these families probably all came together to for the Branom school, which was located about halfway between both just off Highway 11. (Rollins 2002)

Cumby schools. Cumby was the nearest town to the Branom Community in Hopkins County. The first school house in Cumby was a little log structure. The next school was a vacant store house, also used as a place of worship.

It would be after the Civil War before Branom school was officially organized. The history will be shown in that section in more detail.

Colleges. In 1895 to 1905, Black Jack Grove had a college. Called the Independent Normal College, Professor R.L. Taylor was in charge. Later, Professor Curlee had the college and it was called Curlee College. The beautiful two-story building has since been torn down.

Brief History of the college in Commerce (as shown through its name changes)

East Texas Normal College (1889–1917)

East Texas State Normal College (1917–1923)

East Texas State Teachers College (1923–1957)

East Texas State College (1957–1965)

East Texas State University (1965-1996)

Texas A&M University Commerce (1996 present)[14]

From 1917, the college sponsored a 'sub-college' called the Training School, from 1917 to 1948 and graduated many who went on to graduate college there.

Commerce schools. The first type of school in nearby Commerce was probably a subscription school where patrons in the

---

[14] Wikipedia, s.v. "History of Texas A&M University–Commerce," last modified September 9, 2017, 3:28, https://en.wikipedia.org/wiki/History_of_Texas_A%26M_University%E2%80%93Commerce.

Community, who wanted their children to receive the schooling offered, paid the bill, much like a private school. In 1872, it progressed to a part private pay and part public pay and it wasn't until 1879 that public schools officially began.

The first ward school, West Ward[15], was built in 1910 on land donated by Dr. W. J. Wheeler, located at Live Oak and Earl. North Ward, a second ward school, was built on Neal Street in 1912. The building was used as a school until the 1930's. As is true in most places, the size, quality, and location of the buildings have been evolutionary.[16] It would be 1941 when Commerce added a 12th grade to the curriculum and was already in place when Branom school students transferred after it closed.

Cemeteries in the area

Several cemeteries in the Red River County area were used before any Protestant churches were established, because prior to 1836, Mexico claimed the area, and was under such rigid control of the Catholic Church that Protestant churches were not allowed. Even though cemeteries were needed before church buildings, people had to be buried and were often buried on their own property in small family plots. As the area was settled, so came more organized cemeteries.

Lamar County

---

[15] 'ward' was a school administered by the city, while children who attended were 'wards' of the school.

[16] "The Early Years," Commerce Independent School District (*website*), accessed October 31, 2017,
http://www.commerceisd.org/page/History_The_early_years."

<u>McDonald Cemetery</u> –There are 932+ graves including the unknowns.

The oldest inscribed grave is that of the twin babies of E.J. and Mae Shelton, who died 1 Mar 1847, buried next to Laura Irene Shelton.

A pioneer family member and local attorney, H.D. McDonald, reportedly recalled the very first epitaph he saw carved on the tomb which marked the last resting place of Thomas Yates and it ran something like this:

"Remember young man as you pass by,

That as you are now, so once was I,

But as I am, so you must be,

Therefore, prepare to follow me."

Apparently, it was a custom in those days to make every epitaph a sort of call to duty or preparation for your death, and there is in all of them a plaintive and homely eloquence which beatifically depicted the spirit of the time and pious cast of mind so characteristic of the Texan families who settled the area.

McDonald's father, Henry G. McDonald, was a pioneer physician in the Red River County area.

McDonald's brother, who fought for the confederacy, and a bachelor banker in the Paris/Clarksville area, donated a large part of his estate ($850,000 - the bulk of his fortune) to the University of Texas to build an observatory because of his interest in astronomy. Perhaps you have visited the McDonald's Observatory in Ft. Davis, Texas.

Delta County

Charleston Cemetery – is an old cemetery located in Delta County near Cooper. There are 598+ graves including the unknowns.

Union Grove Cemetery - Several Helms relatives buried here, with over 190 graves.

Hopkins County

Emblem Cemetery – in the Emblem Community off State Highway 71. There are over 740 graves.

Peerless Cemetery – is in the Peerless Community in Hopkins County, off County road 4755. There are 964+ graves including the unknowns.

Old Tarrant Cemetery – near Sulphur Springs (also known as Tarrant Cemetery). There are 509+ graves including the unknowns.

Sulphur Bluff Cemetery – is on County road 3550 in Sulphur Bluff. There are 1,114+ graves including the unknowns.

Cumby Cemetery – is located just outside of Cumby. There are 1,569+ graves including the unknowns.

It is said that Jabe Bingham is the first person buried in the Cumby Cemetery in 1851.

A well-kept cemetery, there is no such record or location of his burial and it does not have a stone. The earliest marked grave is of Urbane Alexander, died in 1853.

Mt Zion Cemetery – was referred to as Mt. Zion as early as 1850. It is located by Highway 11 West, about 4 miles east of

Commerce. There are 795+ graves including the unknowns. **At least 74 of those buried there are my ancestors.**

Laird Burns is the earliest marked grave in the Mt Zion Cemetery. As with Cumby and other cemeteries with historical significance, many of the early grave markers were made from limestone and were easily broken, and later discarded, lost or thrown away. Therefore, some graves are unmarked and lost. A recently updated census of people buried in Mt. Zion is available online at mtzionhopkins.com and most cemeteries are cited on Find-A-Grave.com. Appendix B has a partial list of early burials in this cemetery.

The Wren cemetery - located just down the hill east of the Mt. Zion cemetery on the west side of Wren Creek. Reportedly, this was a rather large cemetery which was washed away by flooding in the past. (Rollins 2002)

Garoutte Cemetery – looks like the family first showed up in Hopkins County around 1847. It just 8 graves. From Find-A-Grave.com we get the following description: Garoutte Cemetery is a small family cemetery in the north western section of Hopkins County. From Cumby, take FM 275 North to CR 4732 (right hand turn or to the east). If you come to HWY 11, you have gone too far. The cemetery will be a few hundred yards down the oil road, located on the south side of the road. Drive slowly or you will miss the cemetery. It is very over grown.

Also, they give an inventory of people buried there:

Garoutte, Charles W.
b. Sep. 17, 1858 d. Jul. 20, 1866

Garoutte, Emily C. Taliaferro

b. Mar. 26, 1821 d. Jan. 9, 1895

Garoutte, James B.
b. Nov. 10, 1856 d. Aug. 22, 1863

Garoutte, Michael C.   - mentioned previously as a pioneer.
b. Nov. 14, 1816 d. Jun. 22, 1896

Garoutte, M. A.
b. Nov. 27, 1861 d. Sep. 1, 1890

Garoutte, Susan A.
b. Sep. 14, 1851 d. Oct. 18, 1866

Garoutte, Theodore T.
b. Jan. 16, 1855 d. Aug. 22, 1863

Mead, Ida M.
b. Jul. 10, 1866 d. Mar. 21, 1889

Other cemeteries and their proximity to Branom:

Distance
(under 10 mi
from Branom)
   & Direction   Name of Cemetery

   About 2 miles [3.2 km]

   ENE   Oakland Cemetery - is an old, inactive cemetery of 170+

                  burials, located at the end of Hopkins County Rd 4809,

                  off FM 2653, north of Ridgeway, TX.

   NE   Stewart Cemetery

<u>About 4 miles [6.4 km]</u>

SSE   <u>Plunkett-Pleasant Grove Cemetery</u>

NW   <u>Lebanon Cemetery</u>

W   <u>Stewart Cemetery</u>

<u>About 5 miles [8 km]</u>

NW   <u>Rosemound Cemetery</u>

<u>Within 7 miles [11.3 km]</u>

WSW   <u>Brigham Cemetery</u>

SSW   <u>Sunny Point Cemetery</u>

S   <u>Long Cemetery</u>

N   <u>Shiloh Cemetery</u> – is an old cemetery in Delta County

near Klondike and the Hunt County border.

There are 806+ graves including the unknowns.

<u>Within 8 miles [12.9 km]</u>

WNW   <u>Scatter Branch Cemetery</u>

<u>Within 9 miles [14.5 km]</u>

SSW   <u>Twin Oak Cemetery</u>

N   <u>Gough Cemetery</u>   (unknown undated)

Nearby Communities

These communities were listed in 1895 based on their

distance from Branom (under 10 miles), with the one closest to Branom listed first.

Ridgeway

- Located 2 miles [3.2 km] to the East Southeast (ESE) from Branom[17]

Cumby   located   S   4 miles [6.4 km]

Commerce

- Located 5 miles [8 km] to the West Northwest (WNW) from Branom

- 1895 population of 810 people (with 9,091 people in 2016)

- Commerce had a post office and railroad service

Peerless

- Located 7 miles [11.3 km] to the East Northeast (ENE) from Branom

- Peerless had a post office and no railroad service

Campbell

---

[17] *distances are not driving distances, but are calculated as a 'straight-line' distance starting from Branom. A straight line distance ignores things like rivers, canyons, lakes, et cetera - it's truly a line from Point A (i.e.- Branom) to Point B.*

- Located 8 miles [12.9 km] to the
  West Southwest (WSW) from Branom

- 1895 population of 508 people (with 612 people in
  2016)

- Campbell had a post office and railroad service

Needmore

- Located 8 miles [12.9 km] to the North (N)
  from Branom

- Needmore had a post office and no railroad service

Summary

During the pioneer period, there were several stages of development which can be seen in how religious services developed from providing circuit preachers for camp meetings to erecting church buildings on land donated by landowners.

Before transportation routes became more established, communities and cities were established to serve the rural residents, providing necessary provisions. As roads were improved and railroad service became available, stores and communities benefited or declined based on the proximity of transportation developments.

A Cumberland Presbyterian minister in Texas, replying to a letter of inquiry from a minister in the East who was preaching for another denomination, said, "There is a great field for the Cumberland Presbyterian Church in Texas, and workers are needed. .. But the preacher who succeeds in our church in Texas must have the spirit of the pioneers. He must be willing to make many sacrifices and self-denials." (T. H. Campbell 2017) During the period of pioneer settlement, the same was true for the settlers as well.

4 OLD SETTLERS – 1851-1870

Those coming between 1850 and after the close of the year 1870, would be regarded as **old settlers**. (Ed H. McCuistion, October, 1995) Since the Civil War happened during this period, it is divided into three sections, pre-war, the Civil War, and post-war reconstruction, over the next two chapters.

Pre-war

Documenting who was in Texas at what time does become easier if they were present during the 1850 Census. More records exist for this time than before in the state. We can not only match surnames but are able to match first names of other family members as time passes. Up to this point, we identified less than 35 family names of Pathfinders and Pioneers. With the use of the 1850 census, we can easily document who was living in Hopkins County.

In addition, we have access to existing church records and other works of history. For example, using records from the Mt Zion Cumberland Presbyterian Church, we can document who was in the Branom Community when and build information around that from other ancestry records. Local fraternal organizations also kept records, but must be accessed through the local lodge, unless otherwise listed on the internet. Additionally, membership was often recorded on the grave markers of members and appear in cemeteries and/or internet sites such as Find-A-Grave (FAG).

Because of the influx of people into the area, we now begin to look at the families in broader terms, such as the Finley family, referring to them as a pathfinder family, the Matthews family as a pioneer family, and old settler family for those who appeared in the Community during the period from 1851 (pre-war) through 1870 (reconstruction).

1851 - Masonic Lodges. Tarrant, the first County seat, became a thriving village and at its best had a population of about 300 people. The first Masonic Lodge in the County was organized there in 1851. This was the parent lodge of all the lodges in this part of the state. In April 1852, they recommended the petition for a lodge at Greenville; in June 1852, they recommended a lodge at Quitman; in January 1854, they recommended a lodge in Black Jack Grove, now Cumby, and made the same recommendation in September 1855; in August 1856, they recommended a lodge at Veal's Store or White Oak, Hopkins County. This place was afterwards known as Lollar's Store. It was about eight miles east of Sulphur Springs on the Jefferson road. In June 1853, petition was filed for a lodge at Sulphur Springs but was refused because it was only five miles from Tarrant and in a new and sparsely settled section. The petition was renewed, and the lodge recommended in December 1856. Sulphur Springs failed in getting a dispensation on that recommendation and in December 1857 another recommendation was made.

As mentioned, the Masonic Lodge was chartered in Black Jack Grove in January 24, 1856 as Hopkins Lodge No. 180. D.W. Cole, local developer and merchant served as Worship Master 10 times. The first building owned by the lodge was erected in 1860, the lot being donated by D.W. Cole. From 1856 to 1860, they met in the open by moonlight on top of a knoll one mile north of town, on a farm owned by Mr. Cole. (Tuck undated) It was known as a lunar lodge, meaning that they met on a Saturday night on or before a full moon each month.

<u>Postmasters - 1848</u>. Another source of records were the people who served as postmaster for the area. Mail for the Branom Community was delivered out of Cumby, formerly Black Jack Grove. Dates and names of postmasters for this post office are:

1848-1854 – John W. Matthews

1854-1855 – B.W. Cawden

1855 – J.D. Cole

1855-1858 – Jas. M. Brown

1858- 1861 – Thomas J. Cate

1861-1866 – J.T. Cate (CSA)

1866-1872- J.W. Hendon

During these days the postmaster's job was a political appointment. So, knowledge and effectiveness was not considered, as the case with a civil service job these days.

<u>More history of the Mt. Zion Presbyterian church.</u> Through church records, we can document who was living and serving in the Branom Community during this period.

1854 – <u>H.B.W. Burns</u> was mentioned as trustee for the Presbyterians in deeds made to the Methodist and Presbyterian churches jointly in 1858. From then to 1967, there were Burns on the membership roll of the churches, many who were both pillars and ardent workers. (Butler) 1967)

<u>1859-65 – Harvey McClinton</u>. It is <u>not</u> known that he served as pastor at Mt. Zion, be we know he was ordained as a Cumberland Presbyterian clergyman while still living in Arkansas. He was from

Hempstead, Arkansas (just northeast of Texarkana) and married Syntha Jane BAIRD. They both came from families that were considered of Scots-Irish descent. They had family living in Titus and Hopkins County before he moved here with his wife (at least by 1859). Harvey died on November 25, 1865 in Hopkins County and is buried in the Mt Zion Cemetery, Southwest section, Row 1, Gravesite 5 in an unmarked grave. His marker was a flat limestone slab that has been knocked down and broken into several pieces. A small stone identifying his grave has been placed to mark his gravesite.

Dates ordained: Deacons and Elders *[18]

1850 – David-II Finley, John S. Rucker, Franklin Marrs – all from pioneer families.

1858 – On December 24th, David-II Finley gave the first land, two acres, on which to build a church home. The deed states, the two acres is part of the home place 'on which I now live'. Just ten days later, Nicholas Harlow gave an additional acre joining the other two. The deed states that it was from the John S. Rucker survey. This gives the reader a pretty good idea of where the land was located on old County maps. Remember, Mary HARLOW Rucker, wife of another early landowner, was also an early church member. (M. A. Butler) 1967)

1859 – Samuel Jackson Burns * - He is a son of Rev. Laird Burns, a pioneer family. Samuel married Elizabeth Elender BURKE in Titus County and moved to Hopkins County shortly afterwards. They were both from Cooper County, Missouri. When the Civil War

---

[18] The asterisk marks people who also served as church clerks since the record book burned in 1876.

broke out, he served in the 10th Cavalry Regiment Texas. Samuel died circa 1888 and is buried with his wife in the Mt. Zion Cemetery.

A child of Samuel and Elizabeth Ellenor Burke, James Madison Burns, married our great-aunt, Ella RAINES, grandmother Haddock's sister and their son Homer Milton Burns married our great-aunt, Cora Etta PIPKIN, who was grandpa G. A. Pipkin's sister.

Others who served as church clerks:

G. W. Halbrook – Was the son of Katherine FINLEY Halbrook and John Melton Halbrook. A Daniel Halbrook(s) owned several large tracts of land along the South Sulphur border in the Branom Community, according to the old map. Also, a H.J. Halbrook was listed as obtaining an early liquor license in Cumby.

Ella RAINES (Mrs. Jim Burns), J.M. Burns, Jim M. Burns – They were a husband/wife team that alternately served 3 separate times. He was the son of Samuel Burns and she was the daughter of John Raines and Mattie YATES Raines. They eventually moved to Kingsville, Kleberg County where she died.

William Marcus Garoutte – from the Margaret CAMERON Garoutte and Michael Garoutte family already mentioned. He moved away and died in Hale County.

Lizzie Carpenter (Mrs. Merrit Smith) – He was the son of Henry Edward Smith and Julia Ann BRANOM Smith and she was the daughter of Richard Carpenter and Margaret PRIM Smith.

1869. Henry Edward Smith family. He was found in Hopkins County when he married Julia Ann BRANOM and is listed on the

1870 census.

Early 1850's – <u>Matthias 'Matt' Ward</u> family. Shows up in Texas with birth of one of his sons. Lived around Branom Community during the late 1800's. The Wards married into the Moore and Packard families.

<u>Sanford D. Riley</u> – and his wife, Julia lived in the Community a few years and moved on to west Texas, near Paducah, where he died.

<u>James Robert Alexander Herman</u>- wife, Martha J <u>LITTRELL</u> Herman who were parents of Rev. Jesse Pierce Herman. They were from Alabama and are buried in the Cumby Cemetery.

Their children married into the Deakins, Mangum, Moore and Butler families.

<u>Edith Boucher</u> – didn't marry until later in life to Charley Cravens, who was a widower and operated a country store in the Branom Community. She had already moved out of the Community when they got together. They later divorced.

<u>1850's - Henry Bingham.</u>

<u>1853 - William M Cameron</u> – Migrated from Nova Scotia, Canada to Boston on 4 Apr 1850. Shows up in Texas when William Cameron married <u>Mary Elizabeth Ritchey</u> in Hopkins, Texas, on April 12, 1853, when he was 37 years old and her second husband. He may be the person who migrated the farthest to settle in Hopkins County. He is buried in the Oakland Cemetery near Ridgeway. His great grandson was Gerald 'Dale' Cameron, who once lived on the Cumby Highway on the Lytle place in the Branom Community before moving to Commerce.

There are several descendants of the Cameron family buried

in the Mt. Zion cemetery.

<u>1856 - John Allen Raines</u>. Moved to Texas from Kentucky with his family when about 11 years old and settled in what was then called, Red River County. Some reported that they were originally from Scotland, but documents show they also lived in England. (Rollins 2002)

On November 28, 1871 at 25, he married Martha Elizabeth 'Mattie' YATES, a pioneer family. When they moved into the Branom Community, they bought land adjoining church property on the east. They joined the church with their two children, Ella and Minnie, on July 30, 1894. He was later voted a church elder in the Cumberland Presbyterian church. He was **my great grandfather**.

John Raines, his father from Kentucky, came to Texas by way of Clarksville and was listed on the 1860 Census living in Red River County, working as a blacksmith. John Allen was about 15 years old. When he registered to vote at 21, John Allen said he'd been living in Texas 11 years, which would put him moving to Texas in 1856. John Allen's wife, Mattie YATES Raines, daughter of Thomas Keelin Yates, was born in Indian Territory and moved to Texas near Paris by the time she was three.

She was orphaned when both her parents (Thomas Keelin) died about 1865 and was still living with the Eli Shelton family with her maternal aunt in 1870 the year before she married John A Raines.

As reported, they are one of two families who deeded land to the Mt. Zion church and cemetery around 1901. They not only reared their family in the Community, but most of their grandchildren were also reared here or lived in Commerce. One of their daughters, Flora Gertrude "Trudy" Raines, married William David Haddock, **my grandfather**. They still lived in the Branom Community when she died in 1921. After that, he married Nunie McManus and they had one son and several daughters, who alternately stayed in the area and moved away.

It seems most of the family with the Raines surname moved on elsewhere in Texas. In the Yates family, a Robert Lee Yates lived in Commerce and died in 2017 at the age of 85. Reportedly, there are other descendants of the Yates family still living around Paris, Texas.

In Cumby, the first street north of main street, running east and west, is Tarrant Street, which is the old road through Black Jack Grove, making it the first and oldest street in Black Jack Grove.

The first stores were on a hill near the old camping ground. D.W. Cole had a store there. D.W. Cowden also had a store there which faced north toward Tarrant Street. It is said that Merit Branom was one of the early merchants and Sam Houston would stop at his home when in the area.

First, there were taverns or stores. About 1850, Henry Bingham ran a tavern which also served as a hotel. It was a very crude structure, being made of clapboards. Not much is known about him other than that. There was a Jabe Bingham who built the first mill in 1851. In 1852, Esquire Green moved to Black Jack Grove He had a tavern there for a while and also built an old ox mill. It would be 1867 before a steam mill was used in the area, built by John R. Baker.

Later, taverns were called saloons when liquor licenses were required. The first election on the matter of liquor control was held in Texas on Aug. 7, 1854, following the passage by the Legislature of a law closing all places selling liquor in amounts less than one quart, except in those counties where the people voted for licensing such places. Black Jack Grove had its share of saloons. When licenses were first required, they went to <u>Stinger and Cole, H.J. Halbrook, and McKinley, J.A. Brewer, W.G. McKinley, and Kneiff and Fry</u>.

When these southerners migrated to Hopkins County, they brought their habits and values with them, including religion and vices.

The County had an estimated population of 2,623 by 1850. Slavery and cotton culture did <u>not</u> play a dominant role in the County before the Civil War. The census of 1850 enumerated 154 slaves in Hopkins County, less than 6 percent of the total population; that same year <u>no</u> cotton was reported planted in the County. The County population increased threefold during the 1850s. On the eve of the Civil War the census of 1860 reported 7,875 inhabitants, of which just under 1,000 were black.

By 1860, Black Jack Grove was a thriving settlement with several stores, two physicians, two blacksmiths, and other tradesmen. When the Civil War started, Black Jack Grove raised Company K of the 9th Texas Infantry. It was mustered in on July 3, 1861 and <u>Jim Williams</u> was chosen Captain, <u>Mose Brown</u>, 1st Lieutenant.

It was reported that Merit Branom was also appointed Captain of a Civil War company, but reportedly, he was unable to solicit enough men to fight and the company was never formed even though he retained his title of 'Captain.' Many of the young men in that area went to fight for the south.

<u>1860 - Jefferson Davis Box</u>. On December 29, 1860, Jefferson Davis Box was born in Hopkins County, Texas. He lived in the Branom Community and was the son (who stayed home), of James J. Box (Box Family Massacre). His dad once owned land in west of Hopkins County, right at the border between Hunt and Hopkins (probably referred to as Westport in those days). Jeff Box, as he was called, was also a direct descendant of James Frances Box, an early settler in the County. Jeff's daughter married into the Carpenter family and is buried in the Mt. Zion cemetery.

Some of the pre-war tensions must have been felt in the local church in Mt. Zion as the Garoutte family probably were union sympathizers as Michael Garoutte joined the union forces to fight in the Civil War.

As the tensions over differing sympathies for the north and south heated up, people began to move away from polarized opposition of their sympathies. For example, James J. Box, son of James Frances Box, moved to Montague County, near Gainesville in Cooke County, in the Spring of 1861 to avoid conflict over his Civil War beliefs as he sided with the union. It was stated that about five other families moved with the Box family. Apparently many suspected of union sympathies ended up living around Gainesville in Cooke County.

The Civil War

While it was known that Sam Houston was against secession from the union when elected governor, the people voted him in anyway. By the time the Civil War began, sentiment had shifted. In January 1861 a convention was called for and voted Texas out of the Union by a vote of 166 to 7. After that Houston was deposed as governor and he refused to swear allegiance to the Confederacy.

Little fighting took place on Texas soil and the people were able to continue their customary occupations. Besides men to fight, Texas supplied food, clothing and manufactured goods.

One of the immediate effects of secession was the removal of all federal troops from the state that left the Mexican and Indian frontiers undefended. Second, the state government, as previously elected, was null and void, essentially leaving the state both undefended and lawless. Therefore, problems of a different nature began to surface.

Most of the Texas soldiers recruited did not see service east of the Mississippi River. More than two-thirds of the initial volunteers were in cavalry regiments. Only three units from the Lone Star state fought in the eastern theatre as part of the army of Northern Virginia: The First, Fourth, and Fifth Texas infantry regiments. Hood's Texas Brigade fought in 38 battles and skirmishes between 1862 and 1865. (Campbell 2003) Of note, W.A. Davis, a Cumberland Presbyterian minister, joined as a chaplain and served in Hood's Texas Brigade. In addition to the usual ministerial duties of preaching, praying, and administering sacraments, he played an active part in securing hospital facilities for wounded comrades. (Brackenridge 1968)

Military Units. In Hopkins County area, there were several military units that formed in response to the succession of Texas from the union. They were as follows:

- o 9th Regiment, Texas Cavalry (Sims'), Company: G

- 19th Texas Cavalry (Burford's Regiment), Company D,

- 117th USCT, Company: C

- Hopkins County Militia - circa 1861

- 1861 9th Brigade Texas State Troops Texas Militia Co for Beat #3, Company K – Sims'

- 18th Texas Infantry - Co. E, The Grayrock Volunteers – Sulphur Springs

- Captain Harmon's Company D

Besides his own service, Merit Branom's family served in the Civil War:

a. BRANOM, MERRITT - CO K 9 TEXAS CAVALRY - survived

b. BRANOM, ALBERT - CO I 23 TEXAS CAVALRY – survived.

c. BRANOM, WILLIAM JEFFERSON - CO B 32 TEXAS CAVALRY - survived

d. ELIZA JANE BRANOM - Burial: Confederate Cemetery, Austin, Travis Co. – not sure about the details.

The Shelton family. Eli J. Shelton and Harvey Shelton both served in the Civil War from Lamar County. Because both had served in the Rangers earlier and had military experience, they each were enlisted as officers, Eli as Captain and Harvey as Brigadier General (he also attended military school).

The Shelton family had both Choctaw and Cherokee blood mixed into their family, depending on which particular line and which wives because they had Native American wives along the way.

The Sheltons and Yates families intermarried.

The Thomas Yates family. After his brother, Albert, died in the Civil War at Pea Ridge on 3/7/1862, Thomas Keelin Yates then, in 1863 at 32, enlisted in the Civil War, Company D, 19th Texas Cavalry (Burford's Regiment) as a Private. He showed his occupation as a Printer. Joseph W. Yates, another brother, also enlisted at same time. It was noted that two-thirds of Texans who enlisted by end of 1861 were in cavalry and brought their own horses and weapons.

Around 1865, both Thomas Keelin and his wife died. Keelin was possibly wounded and/or killed in the Franklin/Nashville Campaign fighting under Lieutenant General John Bell Hood and the Texas Brigade or he may have died from wounds later, but this has not been definitively proven. His wife possibly died during childbirth. In either case, the children were raised by other family members, including the Sheltons, who was a sister of Keelin. Two of the boys, Charles Wellington and Jasper lived with James Tilton Yates & his wife, Mary (on a big ranch) after their parents' deaths. However, reportedly they were not treated very well, so they both ran away. More research is needed to solve the mystery of how the parents died.

The George Yates family lost at least one son in the Civil War, 23-year-old George Royston Yates, who served in the Texas Regiment: 23rd Regiment, Texas Cavalry (Gould's) Company: G. There is no record of his marriage. Another son, Wesley, enlisted in 1861 Texas Regiment: 9th Regiment, Texas Cavalry (Sims') Company: G and there is no record of him after that. It is assumed he also died in the war.

The William T. Yates family had at least one son, John W. Yates, who served with Maxie's Regiment on Confederate side 12-21-1861 and appears to have survived.

The Burns family. Samuel Jackson Burns served in the 10th Cavalry Regiment Texas, Muster Date: 4 May 1865, Texas, 10th Cavalry Battles: Fought on 31 Dec 1862 at Murfreesboro, TN. Fought on 19 Sep 1863 at Chickamauga, GA. Fought on 8 Apr 1865 at Spanish Fort, AL. Samuel Jackson Burns. He survived the war and died around 1888.

Robert T. Junell, who lived south of Cumby, was born in Tennessee in 1849, moving to Hopkins County in 1863. He was one of those old fashioned, good natured men who lived an honest, upright life and did no one any harm. He farmed all his life but was for a few years cotton weigher at the Black Jack Grove cotton yard when it was known as the Alliance Cotton Yard Association. He died in February 1907 and is buried in the Cumby cemetery.

Dr. R. C. Holderness was born in Taswell County, North Carolina, October 11, 1827; graduated in medicine from the University of Pennsylvania. In 1850, practiced medicine in Calhoun County, Arkansas, for several years, moving to Texas in 1863. For something like 20 years he did an extensive practice in what was then known as the "Prim Hill" Community north of Ridgeway, and in 1884 located in Black Jack Grove where he continued to have a lucrative practice for many years. He died June 14, 1905 and is buried in the Cumby cemetery. He was a man of splendid educational attainments and was known far and wide over Hopkins County.

1862 - W. M. C. Matthews. Another Matthews served in the Texas rangers, Capt. W. M. C. Matthews (1862 - Precinct No. 2, Cooke County, 21st Brigade, TST)

The Thomas Yates family lost a total of 3 sons to the Civil War conflict. The last one was Ira G. Yates who fought in the last battle of the Civil War. Ira G. Yates, Sr. died August 18, 1865, and was buried in Ft Brown, Texas, then, later, was moved to another national Cemetery in Pineville, Louisiana.

Why this last battle at Palmito Ranch, down in the Rio Grande Valley, even took place is still debated.

Lee had surrendered to Grant in Appomattox Court House, Virginia on April 9, triggering a series of formal surrenders in other places throughout the country. Soon after the battle, the commanding officer of the union forces reportedly wanted "a little battlefield glory before the war ended altogether." Others suggested that Barrett, the commanding officer, needed horses for the 300 dismounted cavalrymen in his brigade and decided to take them from his enemy. Still, others asserted that Brig. Gen. Egbert B. Brown of the U.S. Volunteers had ordered the expedition to seize as contraband 2,000 bales of cotton stored in Brownsville and sell them for his own profit. However, this is impossible as Brown was not appointed to command at Brazos Santiago, the seaport installation, until later in May.

In Barrett's official report of August 10, 1865, he reported 115 Union casualties: one killed, nine wounded, and 105 captured. Confederate casualties were reported as five or six wounded, with none killed. Others, however, concluded that Union deaths were much higher, probably around 30, many of whom drowned in the Rio Grande or were attacked by French border guards on the Mexican side. Others, likewise, estimated Confederate casualties at approximately the same number. Using court-martial testimony and post returns from Brazos Santiago, historian Jerry D. Thompson, of Texas A&M International University, determined that:

- the 62nd U.S.(Confederates). two killed and four wounded;

- the 34th Indiana one killed, one wounded, and 79 captured; and

- the 2nd Texas Cavalry Battalion one killed, seven wounded, and 22 captured, **totaling four killed, 12 wounded, and 101 captured.** Historians generally agree that this was the last battle.

A merchant who had gone from Grayson County to Mobile, Alabama, to exchange Texas products for tobacco, wrote to his wife from Vicksburg, Mississippi in December 1862. He said: *"We thought we had a hard time in Texas, but it is nothing to compare with what it is on this side of the river. I saw salt sell here at $20 a bushel. In Mobile it is worth $100 a sack; flour $45 dollars a barrel, and bacon 75 cents a pound."* **(Linder 1963)**

Atrocity

In what some call "one of the worst atrocities of the Civil War", at least 40 men, suspected of Union sympathies, were hanged in Gainesville, Cooke County, Texas during the month of October 1862. Several others were lynched in neighboring communities. Referred to as 'the Great Hanging at Gainesville', each family of the hanging incident victim has a story that needs to be told and shared.

It is only fair to remember all the men who died in the 'Great Hanging' and remember for their families – spouse, children, parents, siblings.

James Jackson Box was not involved in the hanging incident. A nephew, by the name of John M. Crisp, was one of the 42 people hanged. He was a relative of the pioneer Matthews family from Hopkins County, as was James Box.

Here is part of a letter written by a family member to give some background to what was going on during that time and place:

"… In the year 1860, the whole country became arrested as you know from history, over the question of secession. (Father) was opposed to secession and, before the election, stumped the country against it. He had great influence and a big following but failed to carry the County. As you know secession carried, but in his zeal for the Union he made many enemies.

After secession carried, the officers of the state were deposed, and lawlessness went wild. All over the state and men were shot down and mobbed on every side and property confiscated or stolen on every side without any recourse at law; in fact, they had no law--- that led to organizations in different sections of the state for the Protection of the lives and Properties of its Members. (Father) belonged to one of such organization in which there were about 100 members, most of which were settlers of Cooke Co. and his close neighbors. Nearly all of which had voted against secession and were still opposed to fighting against the Union.

Along Red River on both sides were a bunch of mixed breeds and lawless whites that pretended to be strictly Secish (secessionists), but refused to join any army, claiming to be "home guard". Over this organization they had as Captain one Hugh Boland, a half breed-. He lived on the north side of the river in the I.T. (Indian Territory). On the south side of the river lived a renegade from Miss. named Nute Chance . . . They had a considerate organization. This bunch became the terror of the country. A bunch of them would ride up to a man's house, take his horses, cattle and what else they wanted and drove them across Red River to Bolands-- If the man objected they would shoot him down. More than a dozen thus lost their lives. This organization, as it was called was the cause of the other bunch organizating (organizing) - of which my father belonged.

Boland and his bunch soon made a raid in our settlement, gathered a big bunch of stock and killed 2 men. One of which was our local preacher.... They started off with their property and my father and about 73 others of the Community overtook them and had a scrap with them, capturing the bunch and took them to Gainesville for trial. Meanwhile, some of their bunch went to the confederate camp which was about 25 miles away and brought their whole forces, claiming that the citizens bunch was the bunch that had voted against secession. And was therefore fighting against the Southern Confederacy. They, therefore, held what they called a court martial trial and condemned the whole bunch--and without ceremony or time executed the whole bunch of more than 60 men. Thus wiping out a whole Community and church. They then proceeded to confiscate their property, even tearing down their houses and taking them away.

Thus it occurred that my mother, sister (Mary) and myself was forced to loose (lose) all our property and go to my Grandfather in Montague Co. without protection or property.

After the confederacy was whipped the government arrested about 60 of the mob and tried them for murder----but they all proved alibis and failed of conviction. But I will say that several of their leaders have bit the dust since.

Please write soon," (family member, unknown)

So, we have identified the Box, Matthews, and Crisp families, who migrated to Cooke County, Texas to escape conflicts of the Civil War. We know that James J. served for 23 days out of Montague County division in 1864 and he survived the Civil War but didn't survive the hostile Indians on the edge of the frontier.

Summary

There was increased tension among residents before and during the Civil War. Not all atrocities were on the battlefield. Some people moved before and during the Civil War to avoid the conflict, while others stayed and endured. Continuing in this period are known descendants of <u>pathfinder</u> families who stayed, settled, and served (including the Civil War):

Finley family:

- Lewis and Lettie Finley family.

- David-II and Margaret Finley family.

- <u>Ellen FINLEY Branom</u> family.

- G. W. Halbrook family (also ancestor of the Finley family)

The following identified descendants of <u>pioneer</u> families in the area during this period stayed, settled, and served the Community (including the Civil War):

Edward H. Tarrant family.

Laird (Lard) Burns family.

Thomas Avis Yates, Jr. family.

- Raines and Martha Elizabeth 'Mattie' YATES family.
- Ella RAINES (& Jim Burns) family. They were related to the BURNS, YATES, AND RAINES family.

Joseph Cromwell Matthews family.

Curtis C. Jordan family.

James Frances Box family.

Robert C Greaves family.

Capt. Merit Branom family.

- Lizzie Carpenter (Mrs. Merrit Smith) – who was related by marriage to the BRANOM family and a descendent of the PRIM family.

- Polly Ann BRANOM Young.

- Rachel BRANOM McFarlin.

- Jane BRANOM (Mrs. Jim Ingram)

Michael C. Garoutte family.

- William Marcus Garoutte family.

Joseph Cromwell Matthews family.

George Dawson Winnifred. & Sarah A. "Ann" ALEXANDER family.

Ezekial and Lottie Campbell family.

John S. and Mary HARLOW Rucker family.

Adolphus and Almira Harlow family.

F. Marrs and Julia Marrs family.

Sanford D. Riley – and his wife, Julia moved on to west Texas, near Paducah, where he died.

James Robert Alexander Herman from Alabama

Edith Boucher who had already moved out of the area when she married Charley Cravens.

By the time the war was over, there was enough damage done (economical, political, psychological, etc.) that it would take many years to heal. Reconstruction, itself, brought additional damages to the people of the area.

4 OLD SETTLERS: RECONSTRUCTION

Post War: Reconstruction

When the war was over, some confederate soldiers went to Mexico, while others quietly went home. Others never quite accepted the defeat. So, the confederate army in Texas gradually disbanded. There was a general state of confusion in Texas and the economy had been devastated.

The federal authorities sent General Gordon Granger to Texas to take charge. When he arrived in Galveston, he ordered four important things to be done: 1) The establishment of a military government throughout the state in place of civil government; 2) the registering of all officers and men of the confederate army; 3) the annulling of all laws passed by the state government since 1961; and 4) the freeing of all slaves in Texas. (Linder 1963)

Jesse Butler (A.S. Broadfoot 1967) names the people and families whose memories of parents' stories helps tell of the Branom school after the Civil War. For example, Mrs. Tom Vaughn remembered Mattie Stewart discussing those school days. Lon Burns daughters, Ruth and Mary, remembers their father's talk about going to school there, along with his Aunt Pruddy Burns. Mrs. Butler, herself, remembers her mother, Emma Elizabeth McAnally, talking about her teachers.

Teachers at the school: David-III Finley, nephew of the benefactor (David-II) who helped make the school and church possible and Mr. Pharr, father of a large family of boys.

It was these old settler and pioneer families who remained loyal to the vision, whose faith in the future of this emerging

Community, was so strong that the benefits were enjoyed by generations way into the next century. The descendants of the pupils at that school went on to college in Commerce to take advantage of the higher education, a desire that was planted in the minds of those children by the teachers at Branom.

While a prosperous environment was being established in the Branom Community, all was not well in the rest of the country. Tensions ran high over the War between the states. Indians and outlaws took advantage of the situation as lawlessness prevailed in many areas.

As late as 1866, James Jackson Box and his family were attacked by the Kiowas, James was killed, and his family was taken captive (mother and 3 daughters), the youngest daughter also being killed. (in Texas Near Gainesville) (Moore, Savage Frontier Vol. III: Rangers, Riflemen, and Indian Wars in Texas 1840-1841 2007)

By 1860, the reader might think that the problem with Indians had ceased, but it was only related to geography. Texas is a big state and the frontier remained toward the plains area west of Fort Worth, Waco, then north of San Antonio. It would be near the end of the century before the problem with renegade Indians was solved.

Back to the Box family.

A Solomon Hayes was said to have bought land in the Snow Hill Community of Titus County from James Francis Box. He is listed next door to Box, in Snow Hill, on the 1850 census.

Snow Hill was located within the original grant of James Francis Box. John Henderson arrived in the area about 1840 (apparently also from McMinn County), married Eliza Box, the daughter of James Francis Box, and settled on part of the land. The now-defunct town of Snow Hill was created from a fourteen-acre parcel belonging to this John Henderson. James F. Box owned the town's original general store on the lot adjoining Solomon Hayes' land. The town was located in Titus County, for which all early deeds were lost, but when Morris County was formed in 1875, part of the town lay in Morris and some early deeds for that part of the town still exist.

The Box Family Tragedy

8/6/1866: One of the most horrible events to occur during the early days of Montague County was the Indian attack on the James J. Box, James Frances' son, who has been discussed already. He was returning home with his family from Hopkins County, near Gainesville, at the head of the Elm in 1866 when he spotted Indians at their residence.

Mary Matthews Box, widow of James, made a statement to Captain Andrew Sheridan, 3rd U.S. Infantry, Commanding Post, Fort Dodge, Kansas, October 20, 1866, following her purchase and rescue from the Kiowas. Here's her account of what happened:

"My name is Mrs. Matthews Box. I am about 42 years of age. Was born in Gibson, Tennessee , went to Texas when I was about eight years old. Was married to James Box in Titus Co, Texas, when I was seventeen years of age. After we were married, we lived in Titus Co. three months, then moved to Hopkins Co, (Westport). We lived in Westport, Hopkins Co. for a long time and all my children, but one, were born in Westport.

About the breaking out of the late rebellion, we moved to Montague County, Texas on the extreme frontier. The cause of our moving was owing to my husband being a Union man and did not wish to fight in the rebellion.

It was sometime in May 1861, that we moved. There were five families of us, all relations. While we were living in Montague Co, my husband learned that one of his brothers was laying at the point of death and that another of his brothers had had a leg amputated in Hopkins Co, and that they wished to see him at once.

So we started, and went to Westport, Hopkins Co and stayed with my husband's brothers until they were nearly well: I should say about five weeks. We started for home, about the 10 of Aug. last.

My husband had put a quantity of leather in one wagon to take home, there being no leather in Montague Co. On our journey home, it rained a great deal. About five days after we started and when we were within three miles of our home, my husband saw somebody on the hill, whom he supposed to be one of his neighbors.

He said to me, "I wish that man would come down to us, so that I could borrow his horse for our jaded one then we could get home faster. I looked in the direction where he pointed and said, "Why there are three or four of them."

He then said, "they are Indians, we are gone. Margaret, get my six shooter quick!"

Mary said, "I went to get it and before she could give it to him, the Indians came upon us and shot him in the breast. He fell over in the wagon. Pulling the arrow from his breast, arose and fired at them."

He was then shot through the head by an arrow. He pulled the arrow from his head, jumped out of the wagon and around to the left side of the wagon when he fell to the ground. The Indians then scalped him twice, and cut his left jaw.

They, then, pulled me out of the wagon by the hair of the head, robbed and took everything out of the wagon. Took (the tree girls) and tied them on ponies. They put Margaret on one, but she jumped off and ran around to her father, and held him until they pulled her from him. They put Margaret back on the pony and started off on a gallop.

We traveled fourteen days (night and day) before we stopped, about eleven days after we were taken, my baby Laura died. They took her from me and threw her in a ravine. We traveled on until we got to the camp, where all the Indians were. I stayed at this camp about four days with my children, when they moved me off about six miles farther to another camp, where I stayed until they brought me in here.

I had to stack wood and carry water. When I delayed they would whip and beat me and even the squaws would knock me down. I was very sick while with the Indians, not withstanding, they would beat me. It was a terrible life. They gave us nothing to eat but boiled meat, nothing whatever but that.

My husband's three brothers are still living in Texas. Wade Box lives in Johnson Co. Texas. Young Box lives in Hopkins Co. Texas, Westport and John Box in Westport, Hopkins Co. Texas.

My mother's brother and niece are living at our home in Montague Co, 25 miles from Gainesville."

(signed) Mary Matthews Box

The background.

A native of Gibson County, Tennessee, Mary came to Titus County, Texas with her family when she was 8 and married James J when she was 17. She and James settled in Westport, Hopkins County Texas, with other members of the Box family. Mary is thought to have at least had five children at Westport: Margaret, the oldest girl and a red-head; Maize (or Josie/Josephine), second oldest; Ida was the third, and Ida was around three and Laura was just a few months old.

Mary stated that because of the breaking out of the late Rebellion in May 1861 (Civil War), she and her family moved to Montague County, Texas, on the extreme frontier because her husband was a Union man and did not wish to fight in the war on the side of the Confederacy. Five other family members came with them, but some of her own children apparently stayed in Hopkins County.

Early in July 1866, James Box received word from Westport, Hopkins County, that one of his brothers was at the point of death and another brother had had a leg amputated. The family left at once, stayed five weeks and started home around early August with a wagonload of leather, a commodity unavailable in Montague County. During the five-day journey it rained considerably.

Approximately three miles from home, James spotted Kiowa Indians riding down a hill. He shouted to Margaret to fetch his six-shooter but before she could find it, the Indians shot James with arrows, mortally wounding him and then scalping him. Grabbing Mary by the hair, the Indians pulled her from the wagon along with Margaret, Ida, Maize (Josephine/Josie) and Laura. The Indians put them on ponies and led them away.

Margaret resisted and had to be dragged from her father's body.

Taken were: Mrs. Box and child, Laura (about 11 months old), and three daughters-Margaret, about 16 years; Maize (or Josie/Josephine) 13 years old; and Ida, 7 years old.

Mary related that they traveled for fourteen days and nights before they stopped. (This sounds more like the way the Comanches operated instead of Kiowas). Mary was given a wild pony and it kept bucking and she dropped the baby several times. Finally, the Indians just hit her, Laura, in the head with a rock and threw her over into a ditch. There were differing accounts about how she died, but all agree she was thrown is the ravine. This was around the 11th day.

The Indians would not allow Mary to drink anything. Upon reaching a stream, Margaret, the oldest, jumped from her horse and put water in her shoe and took it to her mother to drink. Margaret was beaten for her act of kindness. She later had her feet held to the campfire and her feet burned for trying to comfort her mother. On reaching camp, Mary, feverishly ill, was separated from her children; abused by the braves and beaten by the squaws.

About ten weeks after their capture, a group of Kiowas came to Ft. Dodge, Kansas, to trade. They bragged about their white captives to a Kiowa woman who was married to a white man at the fort. She relayed the message to her husband and he told the fort commander. A rescue group was sent out to get them back. This group was led by Captain Daniel Brunson. He was able to purchase the family from captivity and all were taken to Ft. Leavenworth, then returned to Texas by steamboat from St. Louis.

While passing through Austin on the way back to Montague County, Margaret, the oldest and red-headed one, was invited to visit Governor James Throckmorton. He kindly sponsored a collection to replenish the family's clothing. He later assisted the family in returning to Montague County.

Here are common elements of the various accounts that were recorded:

- The family was surprised and attacked by Indians while returning to their home near Gainesville, Texas. Husband, James J Box was murdered and scalped.

- Mrs. Box and her 4 children were taken captive by the Indians along with the leather and horses. The youngest, 11-month-old Laura, died on the way to Indian camp and her body was thrown in a ravine. The rest of the girls were later separated from their mother once in camp.[19]

- They traveled while escaping for 'several days' up to 2 weeks.

- Ida was about 7. Josephine (Maize) was about 13 at the time. Margaret was about 16.

- The captives were all abused and tortured, all

---

[19] On one account by George A Custer in his 1874 book, *My Life on the Plains*, each female was separated and given to a separate Kiowa chief and carried to separate villages or camps.

physically and psychologically, and the older ones, most likely sexually (at that time this delicate subject was mostly coded and suggestive).[20]

- They lived in captivity for a couple of months (August 6th to October 20th).

Mary Box (**Mary Elizabeth Matthews Box**) never fully recovered from this ordeal. She had survived several moves on the frontier, possibly losing other children who didn't live to adulthood, and, now this. She frequently had nightmares. **Mary died the following year, in 1867 in Texas.**

Margaret, the oldest child in the group (about 16), married her rescuer, Sgt. Daniel Brunson at about 17, and made her home in Montague County, living with her husband's family at first. They had several children together, including a daughter she named Ida (after her sister) and, apparently moved with him, as she died in Montana in 1920.

Sara, the oldest child in the family, didn't accompany them on the trip and apparently never married. Not much else is known about her, except she died in Commerce at age 72. Neither did son, Thomas Jefferson, who was about 10 at the time. He probably stayed with the family he was already with at the time of his father's death.

Maize (or Mazinna Josephine) married a John Stewart and had one son. She died in Decatur, Wise County, Texas at age 22.

There were conflicting accounts of which one of the women

---

[20] Custer suggested in his book that Margaret was passed around or bartered off from one chief to another during captivity. His version seems to have factual errors.

and girls had been molested. Each account differs, but the story is consistent with the way Comanches and Kiowas treated settlers at this time and place.

In 1867, they were transported from Leavenworth, Kansas by steamer and returned to Texas, then released to return home in Cooke, County.

The goods intended for Santana and other Kiowa chiefs, who took part in the capture of the Box family were withheld by the military government. The Indian agent obtained from the leading chiefs of the Indians pledges that they will hereafter regard the people of Texas as friends, and cease their outrages, and he thought their promises would be kept, so far as they can control their people.

He (Santana) first emerged as an orator at the Medicine Lodge Treaty council in October 1867, where he came to be known as the "Orator of the Plains," although that title may have been a tongue-in-cheek reference to his long-winded speeches rather than sincere praise for his speaking abilities.

In 1871 Santana and his fellow chiefs Satank and Big Tree were arrested for their part in the Warren wagon train raid. Satank was killed while trying to escape. The trial of Santana and Big Tree at Jacksboro was a celebrated event, primarily because it marked the first time Indian chiefs were forced to stand trial in a civil court. The jury convicted the two men and sentenced them to hang, but Texas governor E. J. Davis commuted the sentences to life imprisonment. Santana was paroled in 1873 but was re-arrested for his role in the attack on Lyman's wagon train in Palo Duro canyon and in the second battle of Adobe Walls. He was imprisoned in the Texas penitentiary in Huntsville until 1878, when, demoralized over the prospect of spending the rest of his life in confinement, he took his own life.

After the end of the Civil War, there was an influx of people who migrated to Texas and the Hopkins County area. There were two groups or cultural[21] streams from which settlers came: 1) call them the middle group, divided by the northern Confederate states, who were less aligned to the causes of the south and 2) the southern confederate states, who were more negatively affected by the Civil War and didn't give up the fight so easily. Many were Scots-Irish, and were called, 'borders' because they seemed to be more neutral to the cause of slavery. These two groups merged and bonded as a dominant southern Community. Their identity was predominately southern white and protestant. They were originally working class, kinship-oriented, and historically conservative, regardless of party affiliation.

People who moved to the Branom Community after the Civil War:

1870 – William W. Prim from Tennessee first shows up in Hopkins County, Texas with his family, Annie Prim, near Bright Star when he was 11, after the Civil War ended. He was the son of George and Sarah Prim and brother to Paris Prim.

In his later years, Paris M. Prim operated a store on the south side of Highway 11 between Mt. Zion and Ridgeway, east of the Charley Cravens store. The family home was located on the north side of the highway. Paris Prim died in 1943 at the age of 75 after fighting a grass fire on the highway. (Rollins 2002) The Prims

---

[21] Cultural – rooted in ethnic and religious backgrounds

married into the Haddock and Carpenter families.

1872 – James 'Jim' T. Butler. He married Mary J Beasley and had 2 children with her before she died. He remarried at age 30 to Eveline Sophronia Mann in Tennessee. Mr. Butler also wore the grey from 1861 to 1865 and joined the confederate army in Georgia. Therefore, he would be considered from one of the northern groups of settlers who migrated to Hopkins County since he moved to northern Georgia from Tennessee before he joined.

He moved to Texas with his family sometime before 1872 when a son, James Harvey Butler, was born. A local citizen of Cumby often talked with him about the stirring events of that distant day. He is buried in the old Oakland cemetery, a short distance north of Ridgeway.

James Harvey's niece was Jesse Leona BUTLER Broadfoot, wife of retired DISTRICT JUDGE, Albert S. Broadfoot.

Mrs. A.S. Broadfoot was a retired school teacher who had been active in civic and church work in Sherman for many years, was born on 31 Ian 1892, Cumby, Texas, daughter of late Jesse Burton and Emma McANALLY.

She was a formerly Dean of Women and teacher of Speech at Wesley College at Greenville. She also taught in Dallas and in the Bonham schools.

She was a member of the First Methodist Church, the order of EASTERN STAR and Daughters of The American Revolution.

As in the case of the Box Family Massacre, some settlers in Hopkins County had already moved to the extremes of the frontier to avoid some of the conflict over the late rebellion, (or

Lost Cause) as it was referred to back then. The negative effects of making that move have been revealed. As we saw, the move did give James Box an apparent advantage, since he only served a few days toward the end of the war and was discharged.

Even after the Civil War, the next 9 years was a period of turmoil as the people attempted to solve political, social, and economic problems produced by the war. The federal army moved into Texas to enforce emancipation, which changed the labor system and ended slavery, forcing a redefinition of the relationship between blacks and whites.

By act of the state legislature, the government seat was moved to the current location of Sulphur Springs in 1870, during the post-Civil War Reconstruction Era.

A new courthouse was erected in the downtown square in 1882. This courthouse too was short lived, as a fire consumed the courthouse, jail and some commercial buildings located on the east side of the square in 1894.

After being named the County seat in 1870, the city was renamed to Sulphur Springs in 1871. The new name was useful in the endeavor of marketing the area as a health resort, due to the "healing waters" of the mineral springs which ran freely from beneath the Hopkins County soil. By 1872, a new railroad line had been extended to the town of Mineola, and tourist and settlers were enticed to the area to enjoy the benefits of the healing springs and "Sulphur Baths."

The influx of settlers during this period can be attributed to people escaping the negatives of reconstruction from whence they came. However, some weren't ready to adjust. Some just wanted to continue a private war and were still spoiling for a fight.

Post War Criminals

Benjamin F. Bickerstaff & other criminals – 1850. While he really never settled, we first find Ben Bickerstaff living with his parents in Titus County on the 1850 Census. It appears they moved there from Mississippi. Many crimes during this time were perpetrated not by citizens of Hopkins County, but by people still fighting against change, such as Ben Bickerstaff and his gang of outlaws, who terrorized the entire area for a short time.

Violence and deception: In *The Outlaw Career of Ben Bickerstaff* by Carol Coley Taylor, she describes the post-Civil War era as a world gone awry with revolutions, natural disasters, and assassins making the nightly news on a regular basis. She recalls a desperate time in Northeast Texas when Confederate soldiers and guerillas returning from Civil War with no intention of acknowledging defeat or becoming 'reconstructed.' This attitude created an environment of hate, destruction and terror for all former slaves and Union supporters. [what follows is a shortened version of the story – quoted directly from the source (Taylor 2005)]

"As early as March 7, 1865 the Galveston Daily News reported that Clarksville was said to be infested by roving bands of guerillas plundering the County and its people. By August 10 of the same year the Daily News reported that newspapers all over Texas were commenting on the "rapid increase of crime, with accounts of robberies, murders, and lately, wholesale arson. Men of all grades seem to have entered on the career of crime and doubtless find it profitable since they commit their deeds without impunity."

In 1866 Judge Albert H. Latimer of Red River County wrote "that never in the days of slavery has there ever been known the wrong, the outrage, the oppression that now exists in all the Northeastern counties of Texas towards the poor Negroes. More downtrodden and brutally treated, blacks have no rights whatever that are respected." The same conditions prevailed in Bowie, Fannin, Lamar and other surrounding counties.

Mistreatment of freedmen. Traveling through twenty-nine counties in eastern and northeastern Texas, Freedman's Bureau inspector William H. Sinclair reported that for the Union man and the freed people of northern Texas life was pandemonium itself. Beaten daily and shot indiscriminately by gangs of cutthroats that infested the County, the two groups received no protection. Civil law was dead; sheriffs and judges watched while murderers came and went at will. Another Bureau official C. S. Roberts wrote later that after a trip to Clarksville that outlaws ravaged the area even before the appearance of the Ku Klux Klan in mid to late 1867. He acknowledged difficulty ferreting out reliable information about these lawless men, determining their whereabouts and tracking their movements. A network of spies, friends and allies, along with many intimidated citizens, kept them apprised of any and all arrest attempts. No criminal had been convicted in over a year and there had been only one conviction in the (past) decade for a capital crime (horse stealing). These outlaws did not rob banks, trains or other institutions. They preyed on freedmen, Union men, and Union Army personnel, those who were involved with changing the racial and class status quo of the area.

Predisposed to violence. Many believe that there was a predisposition to violence in the region (especially following the Civil War). Shootings, brawls and whiskey enhanced that inclination toward conflict. Loss of loved ones during the war left

131

unresolved anger and grief. One of these lawless men was Benjamin F. Bickerstaff from Grey Rock in Titus County, located south of Clarksville. The twenty-one-year-old Bickerstaff was considered a hotshot eager for war when he and his brother volunteered in the Titus Guards to join Colonel William C. Young's regiment of Texas State Troops for the purpose of invading the Indian Territory and capturing the three federal forts there while convincing the Five Civilized Tribes of their need to join the Confederate State of America.

In May 1861 the men moved across the Red River for their first taste of war. The regiment returned to Cooke County in late September where most of the men were mustered in to the 3rd, 6th, 9th, and 11th Texas Cavalries. While the Bickerstaff brothers became part of Co. H, 11th Texas Cavalry, many of the men with whom they served in Indian Territory became members of Sul Ross's Brigade but later followed the desperado Bickerstaff after the war.

The 11th Texas Cavalry was separated from the other three regiments after the Battle of Pea Ridge in Arkansas and became part of the Army of Tennessee. Taking part in the battle at Murfreesboro, Ben Bickerstaff was seriously wounded. He later rejoined his unit in the Tennessee-North Carolina border area where the first known accounts of his viciousness were reported. Tales from former company members indicate that while on forage patrols, Bickerstaff made his white victims either stand in scalding water or held their feet to a fire to make them tell where any valuables might be hidden. About this time he was demoted from rank of Forage Sergeant to that of Private.

While on patrol in the mountains of East Tennessee in late January 1864, Ben Bickerstaff was captured by the Union Army near

Sevierville and sent to Rock Island Prisoner of War Camp. Little is known about Bickerstaff's POW experience except that he was scheduled for transfer to Point Lookout, Maryland for exchange on March 29, 1865 along with 500 other POWs.

Military service records cease. There is no parole record or oath of allegiance. It can be speculated that Bickerstaff never got on the train to Point Lookout but made his way South through Missouri, Arkansas and Louisiana.

Reports of the day and the only surviving photograph indicate that Ben Bickerstaff was a small man with blonde hair and fair skin who liked to dress up and frequently wore bow ties. It is said that he could be a true gentleman with the most civil manners. With his looks, manners and experience in foraging, he likely would have been able to charm or steal his way into clothing, food and a horse. By spring of 1865 he was riding with Cullen Montgomery Baker and Ben Griffith in Arkansas and the extreme northeastern counties of Texas.

Local history tales in Titus County indicate that Bickerstaff killed a freedman in or near Shreveport and had to cross into Texas for safety. The Galveston Daily News in the spring of 1865 reported that Federal Troops had arrived in Shreveport and the city was glad to be rid of the Texans who had robbed and murdered as well as created an environment of lawlessness there.

The tax rolls for Titus County in 1866 indicate that Seaborn Bickerstaff gave his son Ben 350 acres of land as he had done for his older son before the war. Perhaps the family hoped that young Ben would settle down. By 1868 Ben had acquired 721 acres of land in southwestern Titus County where he paid taxes on horses. Brother James who had been regimental butcher during the war now operated a saw mill; the parents, from all indications, were respected members of Grey Rock society. Seaborn Bickerstaff was a member of the Grey Rock Masonic Lodge from 1857 to 1867. He was a carpenter until the mid-1850s when he inherited a large amount of land from his two older brothers, both early Titus County pioneers.

Thickets of Northeast Texas. Yet Ben continued his running with Cullen Baker and Ben Griffith and became acquainted with Bob Lee of the Corners Area of Hunt, Fannin, Grayson and Collin Counties along with lesser known cutthroats. Baker, Bickerstaff and Lee would become known as the 'Unholy Triumvirate' 22throughout the region. Until the arrival of Federal Troops in 1867, the northeast corner of Texas was virtually without civil or criminal law enforcement.

Attitude[23]. The general consensus, expressed by the Navarro County judge was that 5 these men were "Confederate soldiers, Southern gentlemen and all they had done was kill 'niggers'".

To counter this attitude, Brevet Major General J. J. Reynolds, U. S. Commanding Adjutant General, recommended that "Union troops be stationed at many County seats, until by their presence, and aid if necessary, the civil law can be placed in the hands of reliable officers, and executed. This will be the work of years, and will be fully accomplished by an increase of population."

One of the first places occupied by Federal troops was Mount

---

[22] a political regime ruled or dominated by three powerful individuals

[23] When someone acts like they think and believe something, in this case, no intention of acknowledging defeat or becoming reconstructed or ceasing to make war, especially over the racial issue.

Pleasant, County seat of Titus County. Major Samuel H. Starr and his men of the 6th U. S. Cavalry arrived in 1867. Starr reported in November that it was expedient to evacuate all freedmen from the area before they were completely annihilated. In his January report, Starr acknowledged no change for the better. The disloyal element "has a confident expectation of soon being able to re-enslave the freedmen." Starr expected another rebellion at "no distant date."

By this time, Ben Bickerstaff had moved his gang from Titus County to the thickets of White Oak Creek just north of the present-day Sulphur Springs in Hopkins County. From this point they were able to range the entire area of Northeast Texas. Throughout the area, friends and allies, along with those persons he and his gang had intimidated into abetting them, fed the outlaws, warned of danger, provided horses and forage and safeguarded them. The thickets provided an ideal hiding place where few ever ventured for fear of outlaws or of becoming lost.

An interesting story was told to Judge L. L. Bowman of Hunt County in the 1920s by an attorney in Delta County. It seems the attorney was a small child in the late 1860s living on the family farm that included twenty acres of orchards and vineyards. It was his duty to take food from the family kitchen, place it inside his shirt, go to the vineyard and place the food in a hand if one appeared out of the grapevines. The attorney attributed the "hand" to Lige Guest, Simp Dixon, Bob Lee or Ben Bickerstaff.

Race war. In June of <u>1868</u> Bickerstaff and members of his gang robbed six blacks in Navarro County, were arrested and jailed in Corsicana but released because no Justice of the Peace would indict them. They then robbed five more black families, stole four horses and shot two blacks. After July 4th, Bickerstaff was back in

Hopkins County where Joe Easley, Freedmen's Bureau Agent, reported a race war on with Bickerstaff heading it. This time women and children were being killed as well as freedmen and Unionists. The wounded died for lack of medical care as local doctors were either afraid to treat blacks or would not treat them of their own volition.

Ben Bickerstaff is reported to have met an older freedman in the vicinity of Grey Rock and told him to spread the word that thereafter he would kill any former slaves not working in Titus County. During the same period Bickerstaff killed several freedmen in Grey Rock and massacred a house full of freedmen along Cypress Creek.

Unionist Lige Reynolds lived in Hopkins County west of Sulphur Springs prior to the war. In 1862 he made his way to New Orleans to enlist in the Union Army as his beliefs would not allow him to embrace the Confederacy. After the war he returned to his family and farm in Hopkins County. On one occasion after making a trip into Sulphur Springs he was attacked on his return home. Reynolds was found four days later in the thickets shot in the back with his faithful dog beside him. Bickerstaff and his men were suspects but no evidence was produced and the case dropped.

The gray fox of northeast Texas. On August 10, 1868 Company H of the 6th U. S. Cavalry from Fort Richardson, south of Jacksboro, arrived in Sulphur Springs under the command of Captain T. M. Tolman. Tolman set up camp in town by renting a building to be used for barracks and hospital, a large stable, blacksmith shop, a few other buildings and a large vacant lot.

Officers were quartered at a hotel diagonally across the street. Four days after the arrival of the troops a report was received late one afternoon that an African American woman had been beaten by Bickerstaff's men four miles west of town. Tolman immediately sent a squad of seven men to investigate. On their return the squad was ambushed by Bickerstaff's gang who used tactics learned from Confederate Calvary units throughout the war. A Union sergeant and private were killed. Instantaneously Bickerstaff stepped up his attacks on the Federal troops. Tolman reported at the end of August that the desperados in the vicinity had openly declared war and called on citizens to either side with the United States Government or join them.

On August 15, Bickerstaff and his men attacked a train of commissary wagons outside Sulphur Springs for a second time in less than a month. The outlaws gave the drivers receipts for the stolen goods, paid for the wagons and hauled away all the commissaries. The drivers were safe because they were not Federal soldiers, but honest men trying to make a living, according to Bickerstaff.

Town under siege. Shortly after the arrival of the Federal troops in Sulphur Springs, young John Vaden, one of Bickerstaff's men, raced down the streets of town and fired his pistol at Captain Tolman who was sitting on the gallery of the hotel. The bullet missed the captain by about an inch. Tolman reported that the state of the County was much worse than open war, for the desperados, not only outnumbered his troops, but fought from the brush so that he could not send out details without sacrificing his men. Bickerstaff and his men knew the territory and rode fast horses. In addition, the desperados surrounded the post with two to five hundred men who made all manner of threats.

Food, water and wood were cut off. Sulphur Springs was in a virtual state of siege. About this time Tolman erected a stockade

137

on the large vacant lot in the middle of town. Soldiers and officers were moved inside the stockade that was also used as a jail.

Beginning of the end. The arrival of the New Year found Bickerstaff in the vicinity of Hill and Johnson Counties using the name of Thomas and riding with his old acquaintances, Josiah or Joe Thompson and ex-Confederate Major Cathey, all implicated in the robbery of Major E. M. Heath on the 20th of January. Heath, sheriff and deputy assessor and collector for Johnson County was on the way to Austin when relieved of $2,800 in state tax money. The local newspaper reported that Heath and Cathey were traveling to Austin together but an official version of the robbery indicates that Heath started for Austin alone, was intercepted by Cathey who distracted Heath on the road to Hillsboro long enough for Bickerstaff and his men to rush to the scene and take control. The guerillas made off with the money, Heath's two Derringer pistols and watch. Heath survived but came under suspicion as a part of the gang when he refused to go after them even with warrants.

As the winter turned into spring, Bickerstaff and Thompson regularly rode into the small town of Alvarado at dusk to drink, carouse and shoot up the town. By April, the townspeople were tired of them but were at their wits' end how to stop the harassment. It was finally decided that the shop owners would arm themselves and when the notorious duo rode into town, they would ambush the desperados. The plan was set for Monday, April 5, 1869. Thompson and Bickerstaff dismounted to a fuselage of bullets that showered the streets. Thompson died immediately. As Ben Bickerstaff lay dying in the streets of Alvarado, Texas, he told his assassins that they had "killed one of the bravest men of the South." Yet in the next few days and weeks newspapers

138

throughout Texas and the United States were referring to the episode as the end of the "notorious desperado" Ben Bickerstaff.

With Baker and Lee shot earlier in 1869, Ben Bickerstaff became the last of the Unholy Triumvirate to suffer death. His was the only death to result in claims for the $1,000 reward. A group of Alvarado citizens rode to Waxahachie the next morning to hire an attorney to represent them in their claim. They wanted the world and especially their children to know they weren't gunman, but concerned citizens ready for peace. The reward was given to them and used to construct the first public school in the town. (Taylor 2005)[24]

It was in the backdrop of this sporadic violence, at the beginning of the Civil War, during, and after, along with the residual threat of the Comanches that settlers faced, who migrated into Hopkins County. With all this, what they found facing them was still better than what they left behind.

Other Old Settlers.

1865-67 - One of the best-known citizens of the County was 'Uncle Dick' Richard Carpenter, who was born near Dublin, Ireland, moved to England and joined the military, and served in the British Navy for seven years. During that time he participated in the Crimean War and was within fifty miles of the battle of Balaklava, when the Light Brigade immortalized by the Poet Laureate of England, Alfred Tennyson. He was with the navy, and the above battle was only composed of land forces.

After seeing all parts of the world, Mr. Carpenter came to

---

[24] Read at Annual Conference, East Texas Historical Association September 2005

Canada and, eventually, the U. S. around 1856, crossing the Atlantic on the old Great Eastern, at the time the largest ship that had ever been built and being the vessel that carried the Atlantic cable when it was landed.

He enlisted in the Civil War at New Orleans, Louisiana in 1861, served in Company B, 10th Louisiana Infantry and was mustered out with the rank of Lieutenant. His service is documented through his widow's pension application. In 1869, he married Margaret Ann PRIM in Hopkins County.

He served as County commissioner, Justice of the Peace in Cumby and one term as superintendent of the County farm. He is survived by his wife, Margaret PRIM Smith, and four children, as follows:

Bob Carpenter, Kansas City;

Emmett B. (buried in Mt. Zion and married Zella Box) and Edgar, Cumby; and

Lizzie Carpenter (Mrs. Merrit Smith whose husband was a son of William Merrit Smith and Julia Ann BRANOM), and she was related by marriage to the BRANOM family and a descendent of the PRIM family. They lived in Commerce at that time. (Contributed by June England Tuck 1924)

Sometime after 1898, he was awarded the Southern Cross of Honor, designed and given by the United Daughters of the Confederacy for 'loyal, honorable service to the South and given in recognition of this devotion.' He was buried wearing the medal in the Cumby Cemetery. (Rollins 2002)

1869 - William Marion Maloy from Alabama lived in Hunt County just across the border from the Branom Community near present day Maloy road, for which this road was named. His descendants intermarried with the Lowe, Haddock, and Jackson families.

1870 - M. Deloach, who for many years sold groceries in old Black Jack Grove, was born in Mississippi about 1842. He was a brave soldier for the Confederacy four years, losing a leg at Vicksburg, only a short time prior to the surrender of the city to Grant by Pemberton, July 4, 1863. He came to this place in 1870 and bought the store conducted by the father of Co Smith. For many years he was a large stockholder in the First National Bank of Sulphur Springs. He died in August 1922.

J. R. "Reilly" Lindley was born in Kentucky in 1824, but when only eleven years of age his parents moved to Dade County, Missouri, where he grew to manhood. In 1850, in company with a large caravan in ox wagons he crossed the plains and after four months of slow transportation finally arrived in California. In 1853, he returned to Missouri and for some years was engaged in driving cattle from Arkansas to the State of Kansas. When the war broke out between the North and South in 1861, Mr. Lindley enlisted and became a member of that gallant bank of fighters under Gen. Joe Shelby. Shortly after the end of the war he moved to Texas where he became a heavy dealer in cattle and bought hundreds of acres of land until it could be truly said of him that "he had cattle on a thousand hills." He died during the progress of the World War and is buried in Ridgeway cemetery.

J. A. Brewer, who for about 45 years, was one of the most prominent citizens of this place, was born in Arkansas, January 18, 1847. At an early age he moved to this County and engaged in the sheep industry down in the lower part of the County. He moved to Black Jack Grove some time about the middle 1870's and was engaged in several lines of business until 1891 when he and his son-in-law, S. D. Greaves, opened a dry goods business here which proved very prosperous. When the First National Bank was organized here in March 1901, he became its first president, which office he conducted for many years. He was considered a very level-headed business man and all his business ventures proved successful. At his death, March 26, 1923, he owned a large body of land located in the southern part of the County and several brick business houses in Cumby.

He was laid to rest in the Cumby cemetery.

Rev. R. W. Davis, father of the late Billie Davis, was a Methodist preacher. He was born about 1820, and after coming to Texas carried the Gospel over a large section of North Texas. His home for many years was about two and half miles north of Ridgeway. He died in 1899 and is buried at the old Oakland graveyard where many of the prominent early day settlers are sleeping their long last sleep.

1869 – William-II Lowe – was born in 1818 in the Cherokee Territory of Georgia, orphaned around age 3 or 4 and raised by people of no relation - 'bound to' an old man & woman who provided for his basic needs. He probably had little formal education and may have obtained land in the Indian land lottery of that time and place.

Around age 18, he served 3 months in Welborn's Alabama Mounted Volunteers to keep the peace after the last Creek uprising in 1836.

In 1837, he married in Georgia for the first time, to Cansada Louisa Sparks. Around 1841, he was evicted from his farm in Georgia and moved to Alabama where he STARTED FROM

SCRATCH building a lean-to from saplings for a house. Sadly, she died around 1858 about 6 weeks after last kid (last of 18), Morris was born.

After his first wife died, Margaret Elizabeth Jackson married William-II M Low on June 7, 1858, in Dadeville, Alabama, when she was 26 years old. He was 40 y/o. She was his 2nd wife and gave him 5 more children (total of 23).[25] It is said they were married on a Monday before breakfast and she spent her wedding day cooking for a threshing crew.

Margaret Elizabeth JACKSON Lowe, born in Tallapoosa County, Alabama, is the daughter of William M. and Margaret E Jackson Lowe. Mary Ammer Lowe's family came to Texas four years after the Civil War. Mary's father, William M. bought 1,000 acres at Smith's Prairie, 6 miles south of Commerce, Texas. She inherited 60 acres. **My maternal grandfather was born here**. She and Moses had ten children. Five lived to be adults.

Between 1861-64, William Lowe served in Young's Company, Co. K, 47th Infantry, as a private of the State Reserves, Alabama. William moved to Texas in 1869 after suffering at the hands of carpetbaggers during reconstruction. By 1870, he was living in Hunt County, at the edge of Hopkins County line, near what was called Smith's Prairie. He reportedly lost his life's savings in exchange of currency at hands of some banking official and he had a distrust of bankers after that.

He shows up on the membership roster at the Presbyterian

---

[25] It was until that in the 1960's that birth control became available and the 1990's until it was perfected and made available to the general population.

church in Branom in 1879.

Reportedly had numerous break-ins of his home with money stolen during the 1880's. Even after burying his money in the barnyard, someone stole it. It was said, he never let his grown children help him financially.

William-II Lowe died in Apr 1896 and is buried next to his second wife in the Mt. Zion cemetery in the Southeast section, row 9, lot 10. Reportedly, her father is on the other side of her husband and/or it could be just a memorial. The marker reads: Professor Jackson.

His daughter, Mary Ammerson "Ammer" Lowe, was in the area in 1870 with her family. She married Moses Phillip "Doc" Pipkin in 1874. 1910 census said they had 10 children overall & 4 still living. Also, that they were married 34 years. **She is my great grandmother.** They had connections to the Branom Community because they were buried in the Mt. Zion cemetery.

This section contains so many details because William-II Lowe was a **2nd great grandfather on my mother's side** and he has been well researched. He serves as a good example of why many people moved to this Community during reconstruction.

In researching family history, the number of children each mother had seems mind-boggling compared to present day childbirth rates. However, this all happened before birth control methods came about. The Biblical quote, 'sins of the fathers' comes to mind. But the new testament says that the sins of the fathers are on him, not ancestors. Nor was it on the mothers who frequently died during or after childbirth.

During the war and after, the following people joined the Cumberland Presbyterian church at Mt. Zion:

1860 – Elizabeth Dorris (widow of William <u>Finley</u> & Cripple Dave's mother.

1865 – Cyrus L. <u>Kincaid</u>, was the son of Almerion Kincaid who enlisted in Company E, Iowa 1st Cavalry Regiment on July 31, 1861, was promoted to Full Saddler Sergeant on November 1, 1864 and mustered out on February 15, 1865 at Austin, Texas. He died February 17, 1907 and was buried in Sulphur Springs. The Kincaid family intermarried with the Luncesford family.

1868 – M.L. <u>Moreland</u>

1868 – Marlena <u>Harris</u>

 – George, Lucinda, & Elizabeth <u>Campbell</u>

1869 – J.N. <u>Harris</u> (M. A. Butler) 1967)

Other Old Settlers:

'Uncle Dick' <u>Richard Carpenter</u>, <u>William-II Lowe,</u> Mary Ammerson "Ammer" Lowe.

The Civil War legacy remained with Texas churches well into the 1870's. Many rural preachers subsidized their income with full-time jobs, as farmers. Splits between North and South remained sensitive points for discussion.

Summary

During the war, several mothers gave (and lost) their sons to the service of the war. Among those were from pioneer families: The Shelton family, the Yates family, and the Burns family. And the old settler families made their contribution to those lost in the war. Imagine the grief, anger and sense of loss that these families felt. It's no wonder many referred to that war later as the 'lost cause'.

Some served from other states and moved into the area after the Civil War to escape the conditions of reconstruction in their area. The influx of settlers that began after the Civil War continued into the next period and, like previous times and places, often married into families living on adjoining land. From this point, it is difficult to continue tracking which family intermarried with which one. It is easier to say that what is now fondly referred to as the Mt. Zion family in the Branom Community resulted from these marriages.

Family names mentioned during this period are: Carpenter, Lowe, Harris, Campbell, Moreland, Dorris, Jackson, Davis, Brewer, Lindley, DeLoach, Malloy, Butler, Broadfoot, and Prim.

As with other wars, some soldiers didn't settle down and continued to fight the war, both inside and in their outer world. They came to be known as criminals and their lives came to an unhappy ending.

People who settled and stayed began to establish a greater sense of safety and security with an eye on their homes, churches, schools and local governments.

5 SETTLERS – 1870 up to World War II

While transitioning from the Civil War era, people who were listed as serving and living in the Community are listed below. When it can be determined when they settled in the area, it will be noted by their family name.

Among those individuals who served and survived 'the Lost Cause' are listed below (underlined are families previously mentioned), along with their present ages at the time of this news report from the Cumby Rustler which was around the turn of the century:

PEERLESS - W. J. Branom, 63 (pioneer family) - He was born in Hopkins County in 1844. At 17, he enlisted in the Confederate Regiment: Texas Regiment: 32nd Regiment, Texas Cavalry (Crump's Battalion, Mounted Volunteers) Company: B and survived the war. He went on to serve as sheriff of Hopkins County for about 6 years in the mid-1870's.

Buried in Mt. Zion cemetery is Welton Beadles, a descendant of Perry Beadles, who reportedly came from Indiana to Texas with a wagon train in 1883 or 1884 and settled in Hopkins County near Peerless. Those making the trip with him were members of the extended Beadles, Patten, Cox and Arnold families.

CUMBY - J. H. Bibby, 67

- Mrs. F. M. Currin, 54

- N. J Godfrey, 64

- J. A. Crain, 73

- J. H. Anderson, 61

- A. G. Abercrombie, 68

- S. S. Mathis, 62

- R. Lindley, 73 - During the civil war, Mr. Lindley was detailed with a force to protect the frontier, but never saw service where actual hostilities took place.

- M. M. Green, 71 (pioneer family) - During the civil war, he was a member of Co. K, 9th Texas Cavalry, and saw much hard service with his regiment with Ross Cav celebrated brigade.

- W. M. Mitchell, 72

- R. R. Williams, 69

- Mrs. J. E. Graves, 58

- J. C. Woods, 68

- M. M. Smith, 75

- J. S. Slagle, 63

- David Vaughn, 78 -

- Theophilus D. Vaughn, 73 - Regiment State/Origin: Tennessee Regiment: 3rd Regiment, Tennessee Infantry (Clack's) Company: I. We find him in Hopkins County in 1887 after his 1st wife died. Both are reported buried in the Mt. Zion cemetery, but she is not on the census. He is buried in the Southeast section, row 7, lot 4.

- J. W. Hawkins, 62

- J. J. Carroll, 68

- <u>E. Finley</u>, 81 (pathfinder family – this would be Ed-II) Served in Co. I, 23rd Texas Mounted Cavalry.

- H. E. Smith, 62

- S. K. Tidwell, 63

- <u>J. T. Butler</u>, 80

- <u>J. A. Raines</u>, 62

- Martin Williams, 68

- J.W. <u>Plunkett</u>, 78

- H. A. <u>Gillis</u>, 61

- J. C. Millsap, 61

- J. M. Howard, 61

-Mrs. S. A. Harris, 67

- W. C. Wilson, 64

- J. A. Wilson, 84

- A. J. Alvis, 62

- C. P. Trimble, 69

- Mrs. M. C. Bays, 73

- J. W. Winkle, 66

- Mrs. G. M. Petty, 67

- W. J. Doss, 70

- H. G. Marler, 66

- J. D. Martin, 69

- Nancy Low, 83

- M. DeLoach, 65

- M. W. McPherson, 64

- Mrs. B. F. Stephens, 71

- R. Odom, 63

- Mrs. Sarah A. Winniford, 64.

RIDGEWAY - W. A. Stewart, 62

- J. F. Herman, 80

- A. T. Anderson, 67

- Coffman, 65

- W. C. Brackeen, 72

- J. H. Rowell, 82

- Mrs. S. A. Springer, 72

- J. R. Lindley, 80. (J. E. Tuck undated)

The Days of Prosperity

While the Civil War divided not only the country, but also divided families and created economically hard times. Worse, the war beat down the pioneer spirit of the South and was at its lowest during this period. When slavery was abolished, the economics of farming changed and not only made farming an economic challenge, but also brought down the price of farmland. These after effects of the war between the states resulted in entire families moving to Texas to escape the hardships of reconstruction from their native southland. Those people eventually settled again, served their Community and lived out their lives. At this point, we can focus on the people who settled, lived out their lives and were buried in the Mt. Zion Cemetery (along with other cemeteries in the area).

As with many post-war eras, this was a time of relative prosperity as the people established a foothold where they lived. However, pellagra, a diet deficiency disease remained a public health problem for the poor, especially in the South whose meals usually consisted of the 'three M's': meat (pork fatback), molasses, and meal (cornmeal). Since farming was a primary occupation in Branom, diets were supplemented with vegetables from the garden, meat from the pasture, and dairy from the barns.

An exception was the deep South, like Alabama. After the war, it was a harsh and discouraging place. The land was worn out and the economy was shot. Tough and practical people, such as the families listed below, were willing to pull up their roots and move in search of a better life.

On the national level, people were declaring the American frontier was over as early as 1890, that there were no more frontiers left to be settled. Meanwhile Texas was still trying to gain control of the Comanches and making the prairies in the panhandle safer. What was coming to an end during this period was a stage of frontier expansion, characterized by westward movement of a basically rural population interested in settling the land. (Elazar 2004)

Prosperity peaked out the decade before the depression during the 1920's. The production of oil joined cattle and cotton production as a major industry and key to prosperity. However, it was limited to only a few, both individually and geographically. (Campbell 2003)

1870 and after – **Settlers**

<u>1873 - Simeon Haddox</u>. In about 1873, after the war, Simeon Haddox (pronounced & alternately spelled Haddocks) and his son, Eugene, moved with the rest of the family from Arkansas to Cumby, Texas. Simeon was a wagon builder in the Civil War. They were originally from Wilcox, Alabama. The Haddoxs also lived near Pickton for a while. It looks like Simeon died shortly thereafter.

Eugene Haddox and wife, <u>Susan Ann Moores</u>'s daughter, Effie, married into the <u>Vaughn</u> family and, later, moved away to Wheeler County.

Simeon and Eugene are relatives of the early Texas Ranger Captain Philip Haddox Coe and **distant relatives of this writer**. They all seem to trace back to a common relative in North Carolina and, earlier, Maryland.

<u>1873 – Hiram C. Moore</u>. He married Cleopatra Cavender in Missouri around 1871 and by 1973, a child was born in Hopkins County. The 1880 census recorded Hiram C. and family living in Hopkins County. He had several daughters who intermarried into local families, including the Branom family.

<u>1876 – Thomas Austin Patrick, Jr.</u> – Served in 10th Alabama Infantry Company: I 06 Jun 1861 Enlistment Date, discharged 01 Mar 1862 after being wounded in the second day's battle of fighting at Williamsburg, Virginia. He was an invalid during the

remainder of the war remaining in the hospital at Richmond. First shows up in Texas about 1876 with his family, including son, Henry.

Henry A. Patrick and wife, Minnie Haddox

Family stories has it that Henry drove a team of oxen across the Red River into Texas when he was just nine years old.

Minnie Haddox was about 19 when she married Henry, age 36 in 1894. Rev. Barbee officiated the ceremony at the Mt. Zion church. They had both been living in Texas just a few years and may have traveled with the Moores and Patrick family from Alabama through Arkansas where they stayed a few years before moving on.

Minnie was reportedly one-eighth Cherokee and had gorgeous cheekbones. Her high, wide forehead and strong cheeks were evident in every child she bore. (Rollins 2002) There is no further documentation of Minnie's native American lineage. It could have been through her father, Eugene Haddox, or her mother, Susan Ann Moores. This could be a project for the interested family researcher.

The Patrick family intermarried with residents of the Community: J.W. Partlow, Minnie Haddox, P.D. Vaughn, F.W. Sharp, Ella Maloy, Ella Joiner, and John Burns. Their descendants resided in the Branom Community until the formation of the Mt. Zion Perpetual Care cemetery association where we find a descendant, Roy Lee Patrick, serving on the first board of trustees in 1969. There are at least 17 Patrick surnames listed as buried in the cemetery.

1876 - William Hill Wall, M.D. We find him in Texas when his son,

Lewis Adolfos Wall (1876–1935), was born. William Hill/Hillery "Doc" Wall was born in Tipton County, Tennessee, son of Mr. Wall and Anne V Hopkins. Brother of Gentry and McNairy Wall. Other full siblings, if any, are unknown at this time.

Doc married, 29 Nov 1864 in Tipton County, Tennessee, Frances Steele, a daughter of Isaac Milton Steele and Jane Hadley.

He died in Delta County and is buried in Shiloh Cemetery.

1880 - Warren Telemichus Binion, M.D. When Warren Telemichus Binion was born on September 22, 1856, in Calhoun, Georgia, his father, Samuel, was 45 and his mother, Emily, was 24. We first find him in Texas, listing himself as a 'student of law' in 1880 Census, living in Hunt County. He married Martha Matilda "Mattie" BUTLER of Mt. Zion on September 1, 1887, in Delta County, Texas. They had two children during their marriage. Before he became a doctor, he was a teacher at the Pecan School, before it was consolidated with the Branom school.(Rollins 2002) He practiced general medicine in the area for many years and retired sometime in his 70's, listing himself as a 'farmer' and died on March 21, 1938, in Hopkins, Texas, at the age of 81, and was buried in the Mt Zion Cemetery. His descendants married into the Vaughn, Prim and Burns families.

May 22, 1908, it was reported in the Cumby Rustler that Uncle Jim Butler of Ruff and Dr. Binion attended the annual meeting of Mexican war veterans at Waco. Only about forty of the little band were present. Mr. Butler is probably the only one in Hopkins County. (J. E. Tuck undated)

His son, Warren T, also became a physician and practiced just across the County line in the Commerce, Texas area.

1890-98– John Henry <u>Bulls</u> family, originally from North Carolina and Alabama first shows up in Texas with his father, James Henry, when he married in 1869-1870. Around 1898 or so, John Henry bought land in the Branom Community from Charlie Roan, just east of the South Sulphur bridge.

They lived in the area for a time with descendants intermarrying with locals such as the Barbee, Currin, Froneberger, Patrick, Hale, LeFan, Fallis, Fitzgerald, Carothers, and McCurdy families.

<u>Clarence Franklin Bulls</u>, born in Branom, was a school board member at Branom school for many years. In the 1930's, he built a service station on Highway 11 near what was referred to as 'Bulls Hill.' This might be the Charley Cravens store since we know it was located just before the Sulphur River crossing between Hopkins and Hunt County. He married Alice Lorraine Froneberger on July 29, 1920 in Hunt County. She taught at Branom before their marriage. Most of the Bulls family that stayed around are buried in the Rosemound cemetery in Commerce.

<u>1893 - Robert Cull Roan</u> family. The Roan family, originally from Tennessee and already living in Texas, moved into the Branom Community where they had several children. The Roan family intermarried with the Currins/Bulls, Cameron, and Haddock families. Maggie Currin married Charles Roan mentioned in the above paragraph.

More church history
<u>1873 - John Perry BURNS.</u> was born in 1819 in Alabama. He was the son of Rev. Laird (Lard) BURNS, Jr. and Mary Polly WEIR. John died in 1879, and was buried in Mt Zion Cemetery, Southwest section, row 4, grave 9. He was listed as J.P.W. Burns on the tax

roll of Titus County, Texas in 1846. He became a candidate for ministry in 1846. Owned land in Titus Co. and Hopkins Co. Surveys carry his name. He sold his land at Miller Grove to son (H.C.R. Burns) 19 Nov 1873 and moved to Mt Zion where he died and is buried. He was associated with his brother (H.B.W. Burns) in establishing the Cumberland Presbyterian Church at Miller Grove in the 1860s. He was sent to pastor the Good Hope Church in Titus County, TX in 1846. He was given a 320-acre land patent that is now in Franklin Co. and 160 acres in Hopkins Co. They carry his name. As brothers, John Perry and Hugh B.W. worked together in their missionary work. The Presbyterians instructed their ministers where to go and preach. The Miller Grove Cumberland Presbyterian Church was established by these two men. He married Lucenda Jane BURKE 7 Nov 1839 in Morgan Co., Missouri. Lucenda Jane BURKE was born 1822 in MO. She was the daughter of 6.

1880's - John F. Ladd family married into the Burke family also. They seem to have moved to Titus County early on, then migrated over to the Hopkins County area later, possibly with the Burns family. John and his wife are buried in the Mt. Zion cemetery.

1881-1884 - J.J. Ballew was living near Emory in Rains County on the 1880 Census. He was born in North Carolina, married in Tennessee, and apparently died in Texas.

1886-1887 – J. W. Mead was born in Georgia and moved to Titus County before 1860 and then Hopkins County where he lived and worked as a farmer and preacher until he died there.

Surnames of additional preachers who served the church:

Rev. Vick, Moore, G. W. Grutcher, E. T. Neal and Gibbins. These and other preachers are mentioned and otherwise overlooked unless mentioned in more detail in other sections.

From Camp Meetings to Revivals.

Mrs. Jessie Butler reports that each year, after the crops were 'laid by,' awaiting fall harvest, the Community would come together in joint religious camp meetings or revivals. Pastors of the Methodist and Presbyterian churches would join together and invite a visiting preacher in the services. 'Amazing results' were reported as members renewed their dedication and new converts came forward to join and be baptized. Significant revivals are reported below:

Revival of 1887 – under the direction of Presbyterian pastor W.C. Beaver and Methodist Reynolds, assisted by Methodist A.K. Miller and Presbyterians W.W. Warren, B.F. Stevens and H. Fletcher Young, a successful camp meeting was held for 15 days, beginning July 30th. Forty-two people dedicated themselves to follow Christ. Baptized into the Presbyterian church were: Mary J. Burns, Lucy Branom, Emma McAnally, Lucy Finley, Addie McCurdy, Prudy Beeby, Ellen Burns, Minnie Smith, L.B. Rollins, F.A. Rollins, and J.P. Wilson.

Lucy Finley married Edward Sampson SLOAN, who moved from Illinois. Their descendants married into the Broiles/Broyles family and that family stayed in the Branom Community near Finley property until they died.

Revival of 1890 - Presbyterian pastor J.W. Mead, assisted by Methodist pastors Barbee and William Taylor conducted these meetings. It appears that the pastors took turns leading and assisting in each service. At the close of those services, 50 people had dedicated themselves to follow Christ and 30 joined the Presbyterian church at Mt. Zion. They were: Edna Smith, Nettie

Mainard, Pearl Bulls, Demps Bulls, Hudson Bulls, J.H. Bulls, Matilda McCurdy, Jesse Herman, D.M. Branom, G.W. Wood, F.E. Finley, Robert Walling, Carrie Gillis, Coral Rash, Katie Davis, J.M. Alexander, O.I. Harris, M.A. Parnell, E.E. Stein, C.C. Stein, A. J. Stein, W.A. Stein, J. H. Harris, William Ward Butler, Georgia Walker, Lon Burns, Rue Moore, Arthur Jennings, Annie Branom, and Georgia Bassham.

Revival of 1896 – H.M. Pirtle, Methodist pastor and C.T. Alexander, Presbyterian pastor held the revival that resulted in the following new members joining the Presbyterian church: Georgia Williams, J.T. McInvale, Aman Moore, Clyde McCurdy, A.B. Hull, Claud Raines, Sam Burns, J.D. Box, Fannie Hull, Allie Malloy, Florence Woodard, Montie Hull, Georgia Herman, Josephine Wilson, W.C. Wilson, L.E. Moore, Julia Moore, and Montie Branom. (M. A. Butler) 1967)

Mrs. Butler wrote that no pressure was imposed either by the preachers or the existing church members, but the Community reaped the benefits of the revivals by bringing new people into the Christian way of life.

1901 Revival – Methodist minister R.V. (Bert) Moreland and Presbyterian pastor S.H. Renfro conducted the meetings. The persons joining the church weren't recorded but the following names were scattered on the roster of the Presbyterian church: Prudie Brown, Ethel Garoutte, Eula Garoutte, Maggie Cameron, Ella Herman, Jessie Leona Butler, Sam Burns, and Ada Finley.

1906 Reaffirmation Meeting – A Presbyterian event only that reported 1005 members, 5 elders, and 2 deacons.

1920 Revival – Methodist minister Wright and J.A. Gaines, Presbyterian pastor reported 35 additions to the churches.

1922 Revival – Methodist ministers Williams and Carter along with J.A. Gaines, Presbyterian pastor reported more than 125 additions to the churches.

Revivals continued on in the Community well past the 1940's. **My sisters**, Odessa and Maredia Haddock were both saved in a camp meeting revival under the old tabernacle across from the cemetery before it was torn down.

Citizens in the Branom Community who were Deacons in the Presbyterian Church after 1870 are:

1875 – John Beeby, T.L. Erwin

1879 –William S. Branom (Capt)

1883 – J.C. Walling, Crockett Hubbard Walling

1886 – F.B. Bulls,

1888 – G.F. Burns, M.A. Garoutte

1890 – Frank Moore, J.A. Raines

1894 – J.R.A. Herman family moved in from Alabama. He and his wife, Martha Jane, and two older daughters, Amanda and Mollie, put their letters in for membership September 23, 1894.

From Broadfoot's early history publication on the history of Mt. Zion churches, we have the earliest record of burials in this area. Those listed below have no record of being buried in Mt. Zion cemetery. This is followed by a list of who was recorded from 1879 to 1900.
Finley, Harvey - **1879** - When Harvey Finley was born in 1853 in Hopkins, Texas, his father, David-II, was 38 and his mother,

Margaret, was 35. He had two brothers and three sisters. He died on August 15, 1879, at the age of 26 and, possibly, was buried in the Mt. Zion Cemetery, even though no record exists on the Mt. Zion census.

Moreland, M.L. – 1881 – probably from the Methodist minister R.V. (Bert) Moreland family who lived in the Community around 1860 to 1880. Grave marker either broken or missing or both. No recorded record of this one, but there are other Morelands buried here.

McGregor, Joseph – 9/15/1883 – probably moved to Texas after the Civil War. Married Lucinda BLOUNT. The Blount and Carpenter families intermarried also. Joseph was originally from Scotland and migrated with his family and settled up north originally.

Finley, Margarette – 2/20/1887 – she was most likely, Margaret, David-II Finley's wife who was about 63 in 1880, living in the area. If so, she would have been 68 when she died. She is not listed on the Mt. Zion census, but possibly buried there.

Finley, David – 11/26/1887 - David-II Finley, Margarette's husband, died at 72 and is possibly buried at Mt. Zion Cemetery, but not on the census.

Herman, Lucinda – 1/29/1888 - not on the Mt. Zion census – probably from the family of J.R.A. Herman.

Williams, Lovena - 6/21/1888

Garoutte, M.A. - 9/1/1890 - buried in Garoutte Cemetery.

Branom, Merit (Capt) – 1/24/1900

Cameron, M.A. – 2/19/1900

Edna Smith - 6/26/1900

The interested researcher can use Find-A-Grave (FAG) to look for burial sites of the above-mentioned. Also, death certificates usually name the cemetery where a person is buried.

More settlers

1901 - Calvin C. Haddock. – He came to Texas from Arkansas in 1901 with his family via two covered wagons at age 56, so he had only been in Texas about 7 years. The trip reportedly took 18 days and they had a lot of fun.[26] They traveled through Delta County, where the Buck family, who traveled with them, stayed and settled near the Charleston Community.

Calvin was born in North Carolina and moved to Arkansas when he was about 5 years old. He served the Confederacy from the state of Arkansas in Company E, Arkansas 45th Infantry Regiment and survived after being wounded in the leg. He first settled in the Branom Community and, later, moved to Commerce where he died.

With him and the family came William David 'Dave' Haddock, who married Flora Gertrude "Trudy" RAINES in November 1908. She was related to the Raines (old settlers) family and Yates (pioneer) family.

Most likely during this move, the David W. Fallis family came with them since his wife, V.E. Jennie Haddock had died in

---

[26] written communication with Lizzie Haddock Wells to my sister, Maredia Haddock Cunningham.

Arkansas. He later remarried into the Arnold family after relocating to Hopkins County.

<u>After 1900 - Eli Broyles/Broiles</u> family. Moved in to the Branom Community from Kentucky, possibly along with the Gentry family. Descendants married into the Gentry and Perkins family.

<u>George Lowry Davis</u> family. Married into the Stewart and Butler families.

<u>1910 – John J. Lytle, Jr</u>. was born in Tennessee, moved to Grayson County, Texas by 1870 and lived in the Hunt County and Hopkins County area by 1910. He farmed on land located near the Hunt/Hopkins County border just south of what is now Interstate 30. His son Clarence, reportedly missed several grades in school due to having to lay out and work as a farm hand.

When Clarence Lytle married Thelma Clinton, the country was still suffering from the effects of the great depression. Thelma's father, Papa (Walter A) Clinton, had been an engineer for the St. Louis & Southwest Railway for almost 50 years. They lived in Tyler before moving to Commerce.

By 1940, Clarence Jesse Lytle bought the Cameron place just down from the Charley Cravens store on the Cumby highway and moved his family there from Commerce where the Lytle family has continued to reside.

The Clinton's intermarried with the Wall and Haddock families.

Transportation, stores, & schools

After the Civil War, people continued to move by wagon trains. They often moved together because of family and friendship relations. They set out from southern states, and often circled north through southern Arkansas because the farther north they went, the easier the stream crossings were. From Arkansas, they might cross the Red River near Grayson County, and in their search for desirable water and timber and settle in Hopkins County. They farmed, raised livestock, grew gardens and, possibly, operate a station on the stagecoach line from Quitman to Sulphur Springs, supplying fresh horses, food and drink.

There were no public roads during the early days. People took the most direct routes across the country to reach their destinations. This was before land was fenced to hold cattle and roads divided property.

The first public transportation was the stagecoach. D.A. Sturdivant gives a personal glimpse of life during his childhood near Peerless:

"...I was born near Peerless 72 years ago. Hopkins then was a border County between East and West Texas, with only a few miles west to where wild Indians roamed. Those were the days of ox wagons, the old tar poles and the old stage coach.

...The places where whiskey was sold were called grocery stores, usually one or two barrels of whiskey on blocks or short legs, pretty much like vinegar barrels, and now and then the whiskey was drawn from a faucet in a tin cup or glass to sell by the drink, or in some kind of container the customer wanted. The old ox drivers would get full and stop their ox teams under the shade of the trees on the school ground and lay around on the grass till they got sober, then yoke up and go on, or go back and get a fresh supply of whiskey and maybe camp all night there. We

163

boys loved to watch the old stage coach go by with the six-horse team in a long trot and often in a lope. Well, this would be some sight now. I have seen eight yoke, sixteen oxen, to one wagon. Then when a new town was started it was with a grocery, usually in a log house or tent, and a barrel of whiskey constituted its stock.

The first effort at Peerless, which then went by the name of Lindley neighborhood was started in a tent on Caney about two miles south of Peerless, by old man Levi Millhollon. The next attempt Frank Glover put up a grocery about one mile south of Peerless. Here the first man was killed, supposed to be a horse thief. That was the most common mode of disposing of thieves in that day. After that a flour mill was built just east of where the stores of Peerless stands today, by a man named Gay. Then it took on the name of Gay City, after that Hillville, after that Fairland (sic,) when a post office was established by that name. Old man Gay died and Garrett and Kirkbride got in charge of the mill and put in a still and made peach brandy. At that time nearly everyone had a large peach orchard. The old orchards died out and have never been replaced. Then is when the reign of terror began at this place now called Peerless, which only ended when the brandy played out. Since that time whiskey, beer or wine has been sold there five times and several have been killed and shot during those times." **(Sturdivant 1935)**

Stagecoach stops or stations were centered not only around whiskey and stores, but also around springs and other sources of water. Springs were mostly limited to the southeastern part of the County, due to the clay content in the rest of the County.

Citizen leaders began negotiating for roads and railroads.

164

In a 1985 interview about the early roads in Hopkins County, Clarence Lytle[27] was recorded by Jim Conrad, of the James Gee Library at, then, East Texas State University. Mr. Lytle described how the roads originally had been dirt, getting axle deep during rain, and were dragged by a grader that was pulled by mules with the tracks being filled in by hand. Over time, the more heavily traveled roads progressed to being topped with gravel. During the interview, at one point Dr. Conrad asked Clarence how people got to their farms. "They lived on them," exclaimed Clarence, implying that during those days, people seldom traveled and either got around by horses or wagons or walked. (Lytle 1985)

The development of Branom and the County was aided by improved transportation. In 1872, Texas and Pacific Railway built lines to Mineola. Consequently, trade shifted from Sulphur Springs to Mineola. Therefore, stage connections were established between Sulphur Springs and the Texas and Pacific Railway at Mineola in Wood County by T. J. Glascock.

After the Federal soldiers left the Hopkins County area, he purchased the block of property they had occupied, and he built a large livery stable on the southeast corner of the lot, fronting east, with the front end about where the back of the old McMullan Hardware Store was. This building stood there for many years and the stable was afterwards operated by Bib Miller.

Mr. Glascock also built, and his wife conducted a hotel back where the federal barracks had formerly stood on the north

---

[27] Clarence Lytle worked for the County commissioner in Hunt County for many years and eventually moved to the Cameron place in the Branom community.

side of main Street. He had a livery stable there and one at Mineola, and the arrival and departure of the stage was the most important event in the happenings of the day.

The first railroad to build into Sulphur Springs was the East Line and Red River, now the Louisiana Railway and Navigation Co., which arrived in 1879.

The East Line and Red River Railroad reached Hopkins County in 1876, providing connections to Jefferson and Greenville, and the St. Louis, Arkansas and Texas Railway built through the County in 1887, connecting it with Sherman. When Walter A. Clinton, Clarence Lytle's, father-in-law, registered for the draft in 1942, he recorded that he was working as an engineer for the St. Louis and Southwest Railroad. This was the same railroad mentioned above, that eventually became the Cotton Belt railroad.

Originally from Kentucky and Alabama, the Clinton family was living in Smith County, near Tyler, as early as the 1850 Census.

The actual rail was laid to the north of the Mt Zion church and cemetery. Therefore, for a period of time it was possible for residents to ride the train to nearby homes, then stop to get off and walk the rest of the way for a visit.

Cumby also had a railroad by 1880, an extension of the East Line and Red River Railroad. It was a small type with narrow gauge and very light locomotives and cars. They had four locomotives.

When talk began of an improved road running from Commerce to Sulphur Springs, the Mt Zion family had to decide how to attract the road improvements to their area and accommodate the established church buildings and cemetery.

This is when J.A. Raines and Charles E. Brown decided to donate land. It wasn't until around this time, October 26, 1901, that the name was changed to Mt Zion Cumberland Presbyterian Church. This church currently stands and functions both as a Presbyterian and Baptist Church. It also has the Mt Zion Cemetery connected to its property.

State Highway 11 was one of the original twenty-six state highways proposed in 1917.

The Charley Cravens Store.

Charles Conley Cravens was born in Hunt County and lived in Delta County with his uncle, Oscar Mills, (Charley's mother was from the MILLS family) when he was a teenager working of their farm as a laborer. Known by everyone as Charley, he married Brooksie Mae Vaughn in Hunt County when he was about 22. He seems to have lived and worked briefly in Crockett, Houston County as a mechanic laborer around 1930. Shortly after that, he appears living in Hopkins County where his children were born. The store must have opened for business during the late 1930's.

Located at the intersection of the Sulphur Springs highway (Hwy 11) and Cumby highway (FM 275), the Cravens Store was a major hub for the Community. Charley bought the store from Merle Mills (not related) in September 1938 and continued to farm the land nearby.

This store outlived the other Community store east of the Mt. Zion cemetery on Highway 11 that was in the Prim and

Carpenter families. In November 2000, the Craven store was sold to grandson, Roger Herman and wife, Shirley, keeping it in the family. (Rollins 2002)

1900-10. John Deakins family. Looks like he was born in Grayson County, Texas and moved his family into Hopkins County sometime before the 1910 census where they eventually intermarried with the Carothers family.

About 1918 – The Carothers family. Carl and Coy Carothers were brothers from Mississippi. The family moved to Texas when Carl was about 11 years old and settled near the old Harley Tucker home place. He married into the Burns family in 1931 and immediately had deep roots in the Branom Community through the Greaves and Burns families. Together, Carl and Ruth, and Freda, Coy's wife, contributed untold hours to the upkeep of the Mt. Zion cemetery and its records. (Rollins 2002)

1909 - John Richard McManus family shows up on the Hunt County census in 1910 and lived in Hunt, Hopkins and Kaufman counties. The family intermarried with the Haddock and Butler families.

Meanwhile, on a national level, the second frontier stage was well underway. It was characterized by a transfer from cities that existed to support rural areas to cities that provided new opportunities, produced new wealth, and social innovation. (Elazar 2004) In this agricultural, rural Community, this frontier was at least as far away as Dallas.

1939 – Ibra M (I.M.) Mills, Sr. family. They were already living in Hopkins County and moved into the Branom Community in November 1939 where they bought land and farmed. Their son,

I M, Jr. was born shortly after the move. Their descendants married into the Fouse family. (Rollins 2002)

Summary

Continuing in this period are known descendants of pathfinder and pioneer families who stayed, settled, and served:

Lewis and Lettie Finley family.

David-II and Margaret Finley family.

Ellen FINLEY Branom family.

Capt. Merit Branom family.

Franklin and Julia Marrs family.

John S. and Mary HARLOW Rucker family.

Burns family.

Raines and Martha Elizabeth 'Mattie' YATES family.

Ella RAINES (& Jim Burns) family. They were related to the BURNS, YATES, AND RAINES family.

G. W. Halbrook family (also ancestor of the Finley family)

Michael C. (and William Marcus) Garoutte family.

Lizzie Carpenter (Mrs. Merrit Smith) – who was related by marriage to the BRANOM family and a descendent of the PRIM family.

1835 – Joseph Cromwell Matthews family.

1835 – Curtis C. Jordan family.

1842 - Robert C Greaves family.

1848 - George Dawson Winnifred. & Sarah A. "Ann" ALEXANDER.

1849:

Ezekial and Lottie Campbell family.

Adolphus and Almira Harlow family.

Old settlers

Sanford D. Riley – and his wife, Julia moved on to west Texas, near Paducah, where he died.

Edith Boucher who had already moved out of the area when she married Charley Cravens, after his first wife died. He was originally from Hunt County and later moved into the Branom Community.

During the war and after, the following people joined the Cumberland Presbyterian church at Mt. Zion:

1860 – Elizabeth Dorris (widow of William Finley & Cripple Dave's mother.

1862 – Polly Ann BRANOM Young.

1864 – Rachel BRANOM McFarlin.

1868 – Jane BRANOM (Mrs. Jim Ingram)

1868 – M.L. Moreland

1868 – G. W. Halbrook

– Marlena Harris

– George, Lucinda, & Elizabeth Campbell

1869 – J.N. Harris (M. A. Butler) 1967)

1876 - Thomas Austin Patrick, Jr.

1887 - Theophilus D. Vaughn. He served in the Civil War for a Tennesee Regiment: 3rd Regiment, Tennessee Infantry (Clack's) Company: I. He first shows up in Hopkins County when the death of his wife, Sarah Jane Maultsby, is reported in 1887. He would marry twice again before his death in 1923.

1894 – J.R.A. Herman family moved in from Alabama and joined the Cumberland Presbyterian church on September 23, 1894. His wife, Martha Jane and two older daughters also joined at the same time.

About 1895 - Isaac Marion Campbell moved in from Arkansas to Emblem area and by 1917 was farming and living in Ridgeway with his family when he registered for the draft. His son, Andres Henry Campbell, lived and died in the Ridgeway area and their descendants married into the Chapman and Haddock families.

1901 – Calvin C. Haddock family.

1900-10 – John Deakins family.

1936 – I. M. Mills, Sr. family.

In the next section, we look more closely at the families who didn't stay but moved on in search of something more. Glimpses or insights into why they moved on are offered.

6 SEARCHERS – Didn't settle

In defining searchers, let's choose a definition of opposites: NOT willing to settle. This works in several applications. In a church example, searchers are not willing to settle with the religion they inherited or with less than a dynamic, growing church, or with a church that is dead or dying, or one that won't encourage them and their children to life a life of service. In other examples, it could be as simple as NOT willing to settle for what their ancestors left them or settling in a place for which they have no vision.

In some cases, like with the Rufus Teer family, who moved from Mississippi and lived in the area in the late 1800's. They moved away for unknown reasons, leaving the graves of two infants behind. Their story remains unknown. Like part of the Box family, some moved on because of conflicting sympathies when the Civil War began. Others lived in the area briefly and left the graves of children behind with no stories of their lives. Still others, like the Walling and Rash families, lost both mothers and their children to complications from childbirth and the rest of the family moved away from the farm life. For some, it could be determined that they just couldn't make a living farming after the Civil War.

Still others remain a mystery. For example, Lou M. Bickerstaff is buried in the Mt. Zion cemetery with no reference to other relatives. We do know that the Branom Community had connections to Titus County through the Burns families, but it has not yet been determined that she is related to the infamous Benjamin Bickerstaff of the reconstruction days. There are several

Bickerstaff family members buried in the Grey Rock cemetery in Titus County, but only one buried in Mt. Zion.

As time passed and the population of settlers peaked out just before beginning to dwindle after WWII, there will be a different system of classifying people. Switching from when they settled to following generations of people according to recent classifications of generations, roughly 20 years each, will lend insights into traits and characteristics already available by previous commentators of history. Let's begin with the Greatest Generation, also called the G.I. Generation. (Strauss 1992)

The Greatest Generation – 1901-1924

Tom Brokaw coined the term the "Greatest Generation" as a tribute to Americans who lived through the Great Depression and then fought in WWII. His 1998 bestselling book, "The Greatest Generation," popularized the term.

Positives: Survived the Depression, fought and won World War II (WWII), rebuilt Europe and led the U.S. economy to the top of the world after the war.

Negatives: Had no other choice with the Depression and World War II – they *had* to survive and fight. They remained blind to racial and sexual discrimination.

John F. Kennedy, born in 1917, was the first member of the Greatest Generation to become president. Lyndon B. Johnson, Richard M. Nixon, Gerald R. Ford, Ronald Reagan, Jimmy Carter and George H. W. Bush were also born between 1901 and 1924.

Those who left and/or ran out of heirs

The Cameron family, classified as old settlers, are a good example of families who moved on. They came to the area around 1853 and set themselves up in farming near the South Sulphur river. The Camerons married into both the Burns and Vaughn families. For example, Oscar Brown Cameron married Ruth Ann VAUGHN in 1913 and had son, Gerald Dale Cameron the next year. Dale, as he was called, made the move from the farm in Branom to eventually open a business in Commerce.

The Binion family first moved into Commerce, then on to Dallas County and later, to Smith County, near Tyler. Several continued in the medical profession practicing in those areas.

Early 1900's. Samuel Taliaferro Rayburn stayed on the Cameron place while teaching school at the one-room school in Greenwood, a Community of about 250 people three miles east of Commerce in the Branom area. He apparently worked various jobs to stay in school and, of course, went on to become Speaker of the House in Congress.

About 90 years later, they sold the farm to Clarence Lytle (another member of the Greatest Generation) and moved to Commerce where they eventually operated a butane delivery business. From the Lytle history, we know the mortgage was never paid off until Clarence did, meaning that farming was less than profitable at this time. There were two smaller houses on the property that were already established. The Lytle family tore down one house and used the lumber to add an upper floor to the other, to accommodate their four children. Clarence Lytle borrowed enough money to finance the farm, buy a tractor, and build a levee to keep the crops from flooding when the river got out of its banks. Clarence, supported the family by working a day job in Commerce with the Hunt County road commissioner and farming at night, while hauling slop from Commerce to feed his pigs. This was during a time when roads were well-established and being improved from dirt, to rock, to pavement.

From this example, we get a sense of the difference between pioneers and settlers: 1) while pioneers built their own houses, settlers bought or rented a place with housing and modified it to fit their needs. 2) pioneers often had to live with existing conditions, like flooding when farming near a river bottom, and settlers would move in and improve on what had already been set up. The clearing of land is another example, where pioneer farmers cleared the land, removed trees and stumps, and set the soil up for cultivation, settlers moved in and added improvements to existing cropland. 3) Pioneers used different technology than settlers, i.e. horses or mules versus cars, tractors or for lighting, coal oil versus electricity, etc. 4) Pioneers made their own roads across country while settlers used existing roads and, finally, enjoyed improved roads.

Psychologically, pioneers had little time or tolerance for self-bragging or egotistic activities. They were much more focused on life-threatening situations. Settlers, on the other hand, were more at liberty to invest in building and protecting a reputation, which required monitoring for ego-threatening situations. This habit gradually worsened with the passing of generations.

<u>The Tarrant family</u>. Edward H. Tarrant seemed to make things happen wherever he lived and moved on with his family as he progressed. He was an experienced military leader and sheriff. According to reports, he became a prosperous landowner, owned slaves before the Civil War, and, later, served two terms in the

Texas legislature (3rd Texas Legislature). In 1847, Tarrant ran for lieutenant governor, but he was defeated by John Alexander Greer. Later in life, he moved to Ellis County, near Waxahachie. He built a house in 1845 and nearby he built the first mill in Ellis County. Here he resided until his death. Tarrant County is named after him and we have very little connection to his family in western Hopkins County now.

Separating searchers from settlers is usually more complicated than the Tarrant family it seems because people intermarried. Some left, some stayed. Those who left were often the visionaries. The Box family is a good example.

The Box family. Children of Jefferson Davis Box, who ended up staying around Cumby and in the Branom Community were William, Millard, Marvin, Paul, Susie, and Christine.

When these children passed, there were no more known descendants living in the Community, although some of those were living in Commerce and Sulphur Springs.

Thomas M. Box and family, younger brother of James Francis Box, have an interesting story about *searching*.

In 1846, the Thomas Box Family showed up on the 1846 Henderson County, Texas Poll list probably after moving to Texas from Mississippi. Some of the Box relatives (uncles and cousins) had lived in Texas since the Texas Revolution from Mexico. His sister, Mary and her husband, Hugh G. Henderson, migrated to Texas about the same time as Thomas and his wife, Clarkey CARPENTER Box (assumed not related to 'Uncle Dick' Richard Carpenter since her ancestors were from England).

Thomas, Clarkey and their three living children are shown on the 1850 Census in Henderson County, Texas.

In 1851, Thomas Box was appointed administrator for James Duncan Estate in Henderson County, Texas. (Thomas Box is next door to James Duncan in the 1850 Henderson Census). According to the Duncan probate records of August 1854, Thomas Box was said to be living in Trinity City, Ellis County, Texas.

Sometime in the early part of 1856, Thomas and Clarkey became acquainted with missionaries from the Church of Jesus Christ of Latter Day Saints (LDS). On 10 April 1856, Thomas and Clarkey were baptized members of the LDS Church in Ellis County, Texas. The next month, on Sunday, 25 May 1856, Thomas was ordained an Elder in the LDS Church. Thomas and Clarkey were listed as members of the newly organized Ellis County Branch on the first of June 1856. Son, Thomas Box, Jr., and James Box and wife (probably relatives?) were also listed as members.

Later, the Thomas Box family moved to Utah where, reportedly, he met Brigham Young, took on a sister wife (who was widowed), making him a polygamist and was welcomed into the church as a celebrity convert. He worked arranging to have cattle shipped from Texas to Utah and died in 1881 in Farmington, New Mexico. The Desert News in Salt Lake City said, "He was a kindhearted man, died a true Latter-day Saint and was well known in Utah."

Their son, William Jefferson Box returned to Texas on his required missionary service shortly after he was married to Alice Odd, a recent Mormon convert from England. However, he never returned from that mission service, and changed his name to William Smith, marrying Ella Mae Embree in Baton Rouge, Louisiana about four years later under the assumed name while his Utah wife divorced him after he failed to return. Later, after he confessed to her (his current wife) that he had another wife before, Ella Mae resumed her maiden name and filed for divorce and custody of her children. Therefore, this would make two descendants of the Mt. Zion cemetery who lived under assumed names.

Jefferson Davis 'Jeff' Box and wife, Lula Martin Box, lived in the Branom Community the longest. This Jeff Box was a nephew of the Mormon Thomas Box. Jeff's daughter, Kristine Box Wagoner, were still living in the Branom area as late as 1967. The Box family intermarried with the Richard Carpenter family.

William Melburn (Melvin) had 2 kids and all moved away.

Millard Marvin had two sons, whom had no children.

Paul Box had 3 kids, all moved away.

The Box family also intermarried with the Boucher family.

1902 – With the arrival of W.G. Boucher (another member of the Greatest Generation) and his family from Lamar County and by the time of his daughter, Florence Edith's birth, it was said that great strength and interest was brought into every phase of life in western Hopkins County. They reportedly blended in the Community that it seemed they had always been a vital part of all of it. (A.S. Broadfoot 1967) As with many family names, the Boucher name was spelled differently over time: Boutcher, Butcher, Bucher. By the 1900's the spelling of the name settled into it's current spelling.

Sally CRUMLEY Boucher, W.G.'s wife, joined the Presbyterian church August 15, 1902 and her daughter, Hattie, joined by baptism at the same time.

Mr. Boucher was a Baptist and, reportedly, there was no organized Baptist church there at the time, so he attended wherever there was a service. Daughter, Cora, accompanied in the music and married Tom McIntire, a Methodist. Other children married into the Branom family, the Cross family, the Cameron family, and the Carpenter family. The Bouchers also intermarried with the Prim, Chapman, Smith, and Box families.

The George W. McIntire family had been in the area since about 1860, having migrated from Kentucky and have family members buried in the Mt. Zion cemetery.

Daughter, Hattie Boucher, was identified as the one who remained and contributed the most to Community life. She married John 'Edward' Carpenter and they made a contribution to the area that would have made Uncle Dick Carpenter proud. For example, he also served as County commissioner and ran the Community store previously owned by the Prim family and once operated by Curtis Ashley (1938) in Branom on Highway 11 east of the cemetery. (A.S. Broadfoot 1967), (Rollins 2002)

The William Marion Maloy family moved from Alabama after the Civil War but didn't stay in the area. Reportedly, of Irish descent and with a fiery temper, he was a good man, but a bad farmer, married twice and left descendants all around Texas and Oklahoma. The Maloy road, just outside of Commerce, is named after this family.

Those who stayed, while others left

Preachers who served churches in the Branom Community seldom stayed, but some did. As a group, they represent specific occupations that brought people and families in and out of the area. Occupations, such as farming, also led to families moving in or out of the area. Occupational opportunities also had a strong influence as the area changed from a primary agricultural-based economy to a more industrial-based economy centered around larger cities.

The Yates family. In return for settling in Texas before its independence and for serving in the Texas volunteer army, Thomas Yates was granted 2 leagues of land (4,605 acres times 2). He sold the land quickly and remained in the Lamar County area with many descendants still living in the area. For example, he was my 3rd great grandfather, and I was 30 years old before I moved away, making me a searcher, I guess. I left for the same reasons many did; to pursue a career that had more opportunities that were available in my home territory.

It was during the 1990's that I began family history research. Therefore, this writer has done quite a bit of research on the Yates ancestors through the years.

A mystery that remains unsolved relates to Thomas' son, Thomas Keelin(g), who stayed in the Lamar County area, is how he and his wife died. He was away serving in the Civil War when she died, possibly from childbirth complications. He died in the war.

The Yates family lived north of Paris in Oklahoma, Lamar, Hopkins, and Hunt Counties. Through Janette Lawson, she brought the Hammonds family together, and led up to Robert Yates, who lived in Commerce until his death.

The Hammonds family, originally from Mississippi, moved into the Hopkins County area sometime in the early 1900's. Marion "Bud" Hammonds was one of the last residents in the Branom area.

Beside Thomas Keelin Yates, Ira, Sr.'s death left another family of children with a difficult life to live without the assistance of a father. From an online entry on Find-A-Grave, we find a success story about one of his sons, Ira G. Yates, Jr., born Oct. 29, 1859 in Hopkins County, Texas. Given the birth and death dates of his father, it's possible Ira, Jr. never knew his dad.

Ira Griffin Yates, Jr., son of Ira, Sr, was about 5 when his father died. Ira, Jr. was a rancher and early owner of the Yates oilfield, the son of Martha E. (Voss) and Ira Griffith Yates, was born in Hopkins County, Texas, on October 29, 1859. After Ira, Sr., died in Cameron County in 1865, Martha Yates moved with her six children to Wilson County, near Floresville. When she died in 1872, her children were left to fend for themselves. Ira, Jr. was twelve or thirteen years old when his mother died, but he had already been working with his brothers digging peanuts since he was eleven. After their mother's death, Ira and his brothers signed on as cowboys, working for a Mr. J. Thompson. The Thompson family's governess taught him how to read and write when he was fourteen.

When he was nineteen Yates began buying cattle and horses and driving them to market in San Antonio. He was working as a cowhand for J. N. Upton when he married Anna Shockley Brooks, the daughter of a Methodist minister, in Karnes County, between San Antonio and Corpus Christi on January 26, 1883. Not long after his marriage Yates traveled to the area of San Angelo in Tom Green County, in search of a lost brother reported seen along the Concho River. Impressed by the abundant grass and water he found there, he returned to the Upton ranch and convinced Upton to send him and his family to the area with a herd of cattle. Later, he bought a spread of his own near the town of Crow's Nest near Ft. Davis.

Over the next twenty years Yates threw himself into a variety of businesses and occupations in Tom Green, Crockett, and Upton counties. During the 1890s he ran a ranch for John Nasworthy and went into business with him in a combined butcher shop and livery; in 1899 Yates served a term as city marshal of San Angelo and that same year bought a ranch in Lipan Flat, Tom Green County. After that venture, he worked for the National Livestock Commission Company and did some independent trading on the side. In 1911, in partnership with Louis L. Farr, Yates bought a ranch in Crockett County. About 1913, while still living on that ranch, he paid 216 cattle (valued at fifty dollars per head) for a failing dry-goods store in Rankin, despite the advice of friends who warned him against the venture.

By 1915 Yates's store was doing $5,000 worth of business per month, a "pretty durn good" performance considering the area's sparse population. The store's profit-making potential attracted the attention of Thomas Hickox, a Pecos County rancher and businessman who was looking to unload his 16,640-acre River Ranch in Pecos County. The property was unfenced and plagued by disputed boundaries, frequent droughts, and "greasy" well water. In early 1915 Hickox proposed to trade the River Ranch to Yates for the store. Friends such as Nub Pulliam, who had once owned the property, warned him against the deal, saying that "even buffalo know better than to cross the Pecos-that a crow would not fly over it, and it was not worth the taxes." He made the trade anyway.

As his granddaughter, Mrs. Estelle Holmes, later explained,

Yates "didn't know beans about groceries," but he did know ranching and was anxious to own such a large parcel of land. Under the terms of the deal consummated on June 1, 1915, Yates agreed to pay an additional $16,559 over the next three years to pay off the existing mortgage on the land and to cover charges to the state's Permanent School Fund. Soon afterward he bought even more land, including a 3,600-acre vacancy (a strip of land unaccounted for during the original surveys) that ran through the middle of the property. In the 1920s the Yates Ranch was still struggling to make a profit when Ira approached Levi Smith of the Transcontinental Oil Company in San Angelo and convinced him to drill on his ranch despite its location.

Although oil had been found in West Texas, experts did not believe that there was any west of the Pecos River. Sharing the lease with Transcontinental, Ohio Oil (which became Marathon Oil) drilled four wells on Yates's ranch before they struck oil on October 28, 1926. Yates became an instant millionaire. He proceeded to sell oil leases from his front porch and accumulated $180,000 in one day. The oil boom town of Red Barn sprang up around the Yates homestead. In 1938 Yates donated 152 acres for the new town of Iraan (pronounced, Ira Ann). He and his wife also donated Yates Hill at Camp Louis Farr to the Concho Valley Council of Boy Scouts. After his wife's death, Yates erected the Annie Yates Memorial Citadel for the Salvation Army in San Angelo. Ira Yates died on April 12, 1939. (Kepner 2010)

Ira's descendants have donated money to other charities, established a wildlife conservation, preserve, and operate car dealerships in Austin, Texas.

The <u>Haddock family</u>. Marvin Haddock, grandson of Calvin Haddock and John Allen Raines, stayed in Branom and farmed until 1953. After his wife died and left 7 children, he moved away to Commerce and took a job at the college. The two daughters, Odessa and Maredia married and moved away with their husbands. Two of the sons moved away, while three stayed nearby. All did move out of the Branom Community with Marvin and never moved back.

Summary

In this section we have identified families who didn't settle in the area. Some moved away early. Others stayed until later, allowing circumstances to affect the move. Some prospered. Some did not. Again, circumstances affected what happened after the move. Geography also had something to do with it. Some were late arrivals to the area and stayed until their descendants died off and/or moved away. Others, like the Lytle family, arrived late and stayed creating a family that has survived through the years.

One member of the Yates family who moved away, despite a disadvantaged beginning, ended up creating a family dynasty, based on wealth gained from land and oil. Many families stayed and lived through the decline. Others left and came home to visit periodically, probably serving to witness the decline more.

Families, not already listed, that are named in this section are: Teer, Walling, Rash, Maloy, Bickerstaff, Cameron, Binion, Rayburn, Tarrant, Box, Boucher, McIntire, and Hammonds family.

Each had a bit of the searcher in them that took them away or brought them there. A bit of the settler in them contributed to those families who settled wherever they ended up.

7 SETTLERS – After World War II

Those who stayed on after World War II (WWII)

After WWII, Texas mutated from a rural and agricultural state to an urban, industrial one, trying to catch up with a frontier that was already aging in the northern states. This rural frontier had been up and running by the mid-1920's, after the end of World War I (WWI) and was coming to an end after WWII. (Elazar 2004) The changes caused unfamiliar problems and exacerbated old ones for a population grounded in agrarian values. Two-party politics emerged as the state's electorate turned from a near absolute allegiance to its Southern Democratic heritage to one that frequently elected Republican officeholders.

The dominant migration pattern in postwar Texas was movement from the countryside to the city. Statisticians reported in 1945 that some 500,000 Texans left 200 rural counties to join the wartime industrial workforce in the fifty-four urban counties. Farmers were exempt from the draft during WWII, so that held many to the farm until after the war. The 1950 census failed to show an expected return of the workers to the farms but reported that, for the first time in the state's history, more Texans lived in the city than in the country.

From 'Texas Quote of the Day' on Facebook, here is a comment by writer William Humphrey on the changes from the time he left northeast Texas in 1945 to the time he returned 32 years later, in 1977:

"Gone were the spreading cotton fields I remembered, although

this was the season when they should have been beginning to whiten. The few patches that remained were small and sparse, like the patches of snow lingering on in sunless spots in New England in March and April. The prairie **grass that had been there before the fields were broken for cotton had reclaimed them. The woods were gone ---- even Sulphur Bottom, that wilderness into which my father had gone in pursuit of the fugitive gunman; grazing land now, nearly all of it. For in a move that reverses Texas history, a move totally opposite to what I knew in my childhood, one which all but turns the world upside down, which makes the sun set in the East, Red River County has ceased to be the Old South and became Far West.**

I who for years had had to set my Northern friends straight by pointing out that I was a Southerner not a Westerner, and that I had never seen a cowboy or for that matter a beef cow any more than they had, found myself in the Texas of legend and the popular image which, when I was a child, had seemed more romantic to me than to boy of New England precisely because it was closer to me than to him and yet still worlds away.

Gone from the square were the bib overalls of my childhood when the farmers came to town on Saturday. Ranchers now, they came in high-heeled boots and rolled-brim hats, a costume that would have provoked surprise, and even more derision, there, in my time, as it would on Manhattan's Madison Avenue."

----- William Humphrey, 1977 (searcher)

This quote captures changes that would have gone almost unnoticed if a person had stayed and witnessed them gradually.

Staying and settling in the Branom Community were the following families, each headed up by a member of the Greatest

Generation:

The Jetton family. Born in Hunt County around Lone Oak, Eugene Floyd Jetton first appears on the records living in Hopkins County on the 1940 census. He married Evie Marie McLeroy around age 22 and they lived close to Quinlan for a while. Their daughter, Myra Flo, married into the Tucker family.

The McLeroy family. Floyd Jetton probably met the McLeroy family around Lone Oak where both families once lived before moving to Branom. Marie Jetton was brother to James Ed 'Boots' McLeroy. The McLeroy family has ancestors spread out from Commerce in Hunt County to Sulphur Springs in Hopkins County.

The TUCKER family. George Richard Tucker first shows up on the 1910 Van Zandt County, Texas census shortly after he moved his wife and family of seven children from Alabama. In 1920, they were recorded as living in Rains County and owned their own farm. They later moved to Hopkins County in the Branom area where he died. He is buried in the Emblem cemetery. There are only a limited few Tuckers buried in the Mt. Zion cemetery. His son, Harley Tucker and related family lived (and still live) in the Branom Community and are known for their red-haired offspring. Glendale Tucker was a member of the Mt. Zion board of trustees for many years and his son, Buff, now serves.

The Swift family. Lou Ella Swift, mother of Marcille BARRINGTON Tucker, became a part of the Mt. Zion family through the Tucker family long before she moved there in 1981. Widowed, and spending most of her holidays with her daughter in the Branom Community, she was described as a 'feisty' lady who loved gardening, baking, and people. Locally, she was known as 'Grannie Swift.' (Rollins 2002) Her maiden name was Lou Ella Sassar and married twice, had her children with Otis Ray Barrington, and came on the scene with the last name of Swift.

The <u>Reed family</u>. Jess and Bessie Reed moved from the Oakland Community to the Branom Community around 1940. Edgar Phillip Reed and wife moved to the Branom Community in the mid-1970's after he retired. Both were relatives of Eva REED Tucker.

By the time the Mt. Zion Perpetual Care Cemetery Association was formed in 1969, most of the families who stayed and settled were related to everyone else, including those who had moved on searching for better opportunities. This happened during a lifetime, but it impacted and overlapped several generations. Many still had childhood memories of a beginning in the Branom Community and how it was.

Silent Generation - 1925-1942

They were between the two most-hyped generations in American history, the Greatest Generation and the Baby Boomers.

A 1951 essay in Time magazine dubbed the people in this age group the "Silent Generation" because they were more cautious than their parents. The children who grew up during this time worked very hard and kept quiet. It was commonly understood that children should be seen and not heard.

The Silent Generation helped shape 20th century pop culture, with pioneering rock musicians, iconic filmmakers, television legends, beat poets, gonzo journalists and groundbreaking political satirists.

Positives: Many of them still read the local paper, so . . . no need to insult them. And Don Draper on "Mad Men" was part of this generation.

189

Negatives: Fought the "forgotten war" (Korea) to a tie, teamed with the Greatest Generation to oppose baby boomers, gave us no presidents (Greatest Generation provided seven, baby boomers three so far). Elected Richard Nixon president. Twice.

After World War II most of the residents in the Branom Community moved away. The ones who stayed became gentleman ranchers.

An example would be William 'Little Ben' Herman Jr. (1923–2011) who operated a dairy and ranched on his father's farm in the Branom Community. His wife was Charley Cravens' daughter Nita, who was a fixture in the Community, due to the store her dad operated. From the Silent Generation herself, she served on the board of trustees of the Mt. Zion perpetual care cemetery association for years.

Another example, would be Neal and Yvonne Stewart, born in 1939 and 1938, children of settlers who settled and served on the board of trustees of the Mt. Zion perpetual care cemetery association for years.

Lee Roy Pierce, born in 1934 (from the Silent Generation), and a descendant of the Fleenor and Frank Pierce family, is another example of a person who served on the board of trustees of the Mt. Zion perpetual care cemetery association for years. However, he left the Community for the Dallas/Ft. Worth area, developed a construction business, bought land, and prospered.

His sister, Ruth PIERCE Rollins, moved to Delta County and served a while on the board of trustees as well.

They were both descendants of Ed Barlow Pierce and sons, Claude and Frank, who lived in Hopkins and Fannin counties.

Abt 1930 – The <u>Arrington family</u>. The census shows Edward Alexander Arrington appearing in Hopkins County for the first time. Grandfather of Harold Dean Arrington, and father of William Grady Arrington, he was originally from Alabama. They moved first to Wood County where they lived for 20 or so years, before moving to the Branom Community.

Harold married Oleta HADDOCK and raised a family in Commerce, where he ran a concrete construction business. Three generations of the Arrington family are buried in the Mt. Zion cemetery.

Up to WWII, the Branom Community had good leaders and more leaders in training to carry on the good work in the spirit on which the Community was built. By this time, the area was thickly settled.

In her little booklet on the History of Mt. Zion, Mrs. Jesse BUTLER Broadfoot stated that with such citizens living and working in the Community, as the descendants of the Boxes, Vaughns, Stewarts, Burns, Camerons, Bouchers, Greaves, she anticipated that the same high-quality leadership that made up old Mt. Zion would continue.

However, generations have different questions and different goals and values. People moved away. Things changed and the quality of life in Branom began its decline.

A new frontier was attracting young people and other searchers to the city. It was a frontier characterized by a reordering of an already individualistic society through newly invented technologies and a settlement pattern based on automobile transportation and highways. The pathfinders discovered the Comanches effective use of their technology: the Spanish mustang. Searchers, on this frontier, discovered the effective use of the automobile. They could live and work in the city and maintain relationships with relatives in rural areas.

Indicators of the decline

Economic indicators were not only the traditional ones, such as average income and unemployment, but sustainable indicators, such as the number of hours of paid employment at the wage needed to support basic needs. Employment opportunities in the cities were not only more prevalent, but also paid more for the number of hours worked, and enough to support basic needs. The farming lifestyle couldn't compete with this.

Traditional environmental indicators, such as water and air pollution, and amount of waste garbage generated were sacrificed for the city life. When they moved away from rural life, families often left run-down houses, garbage dumps, and outdoor plumbing and water sources with no regulation for future generations until County government stepped in.

Traditional social indicators of the decline in quality of life was most noted. For example, people returned for class reunions and Memorial Day reunions and reminisced about the old days, then returned to their city lives. Over time, the attendance of those reunions declined to the point where attendance was no longer counted. An indicator of sustainability was overlooked by leaders as more young people from the Branom Community who went to college didn't come back to or stay in the Community. Another sustainability indicator would be the number of registered voters in the Community. One could simply ask the question: 'How long has it been since a resident of the Community was elected as commissioner for the precinct?'

Even closer to home, when was the last time you felt

comfortable asking a neighbor for a favor or for help with a project? As a measure of neighborliness, this indicator goes directly to the decline in the Mt. Zion cemetery association when trustees living out of town had to transport their equipment from the city into the Community to perform cemetery work. Other examples, of the decline in neighborliness include a need to employ caretakers for the maintenance of the cemetery grounds instead of relying on volunteers from neighboring families.

Yvonne Stewart Rollins has provided the following notes about caretakers at Mt. Zion:

Prior to 1970, cleaning and care of the cemetery was done by whomever was available and willing. Each grave site was hoed and raked at that time. It was understood that occasionally there would be a 'cemetery cleaning day' declared. All interested people would show up with tools: hoe, rake, shovel, etc. Lunch would be spread at noon for all to enjoy. Since cleaning day happened occasionally, the cemetery would usually get bad before another cleaning day was declared.

During the 1940's G.T. 'Tom' Vaughn was the overseer of the cemetery and maybe before then. When his health failed, Carl Carothers took over the oversight and care of the cemetery. They would hire anyone they could get to hoe. People remembered getting anywhere from 50 cents to a dollar a day. The overseer was there to provide drinking water and to sharpen hoes.

After the cemetery association was formed, the trustees began contracting with a caretaker or maintenance person. Records show that Forrest Boswell was hired for $400 a year in 1970. Willis and Juanita Gunter became caretakers at $42 a month or $504 per year in June 1972. By 1982, the trustees were paying anyone volunteering to work, including Boswell, the amount of $4 per hour. In 1984, a new riding lawnmower was purchased for the caretaker's use, probably marking a transition to cutting the grass, with hoeing and raking the grave sites becoming a thing of the past. By 1989, William Allen Horton was hired as a caretaker. The Cook couple from Como worked as caretakers from 1994 to 1997 and Billy Jack Horton was probably hired after that, probably around year 2000. He has probably worked as a contractor since then until his health recently (2017) started failing.

This time frame, up to this point, corresponds loosely with Broadfoot's 1967 booklet on the Branom Community history. Fast forward to the next contribution to the history of the area: *Mt. Zion: its history, its churches, its schools, its families, and its folks*. Compiled by Yvonne Stewart Rollins and initially printed by the Texas A&M University-Commerce print shop in September 2001 (Rollins 2002). Like Broadfoot's booklet, this booklet looks back and includes information up to the date of publication. This is an excellent resource that had a limited distribution and is highly recommended for anyone interested in further research of the Branom Community and the Mt. Zion church and cemetery.

We pick up in 1967, where Broadfoot leaves us and Rollins' work overlaps. A significant event during these days was the organization of the Mt. Zion Perpetual Care Cemetery Association on June 1, 1969. Of note, was the reference to the word, *perpetual*. In that word, the implication was that the cemetery and its trustees would insure the maintenance and care of the place throughout perpetuity, which essentially means forever.[28]

---

[28] *"It's the only piece of property you sell once but are expected to care for forever." says*

Through the minutes of this organization, we can track the family members who stayed active and interested in the Community.

Elected to the first board of trustees and appointed offices were the following:

Raymon Stewart, President

Ralph Vaughn, Vice-President

Carl Carothers, Treasurer

Vera Vaughn, Secretary

James Scott Buchanan served as temporary secretary. Afterwards James Scott actively provided leadership for the trustees, periodically suggesting the development of a landscaping plan for the cemetery and serving mostly as secretary on the board from 1970 until his death in 2009. The landscape plan was never made, let alone implemented. He served as a trustee for about 39 years, the second longest.

Raymond Fitzgerald presided over the general membership meeting and by-laws were amended to reduce trustees from 9 to 6 with overlapping terms.

Raymond Fitzgerald had married into the Butler family, daughter of Uncle Jim Butler.

As time passed, new members of the board can be traced through the minutes:

Dale Flatt, an Austin firefighter who founded a preservation group, Save Austin's Cemeteries, in 2004.

1970 – Richard Carpenter (trustee with deep roots through the Branom family),

Noble 'Forrest' Boswell family. (caretaker) James Martin Boswell, Forrest's grandfather left Georgia around 1869 after the Civil War, where he served in the 40th Infantry and moved to Texas, first near Paris, then ended up near Cumby before he died in 1905. He is buried in the Stewart cemetery on the Maloy road between Commerce and Campbell.

Forrest's father David G. Boswell married Arrie S Elmira LOW(E), daughter of the William Low(e) family, Old settlers in the area.

1973 – Willis M. & Juanita HADDOCK Gunter family. (caretakers) Born in Georgia and moved to Texas Willis' father, William T. Gunter settled near Cumby where Willis was born in 1906. Willis and Juanita were childless, but raised Gary David HADDOCK, infant of Marvin and Elsie PIPKIN Haddock, after she died. They later adopted Gary. Both Willis and Juanita were from the Greatest Generation. When they did move away from the Branom Community, it was no farther than Commerce.

1975 – Lucille Holley & sons donated land to west side of cemetery (see Holley family below).

1978 – Clyde Butler mentioned (ancestor of the Butler family).

At this time, additional families were present and living in the area, who have yet to be mentioned.

The HOLLEY family (Clan 1). In 1899, John Hardin Holley married Willie Ophelia YOUNG and they were living in Fannin County when their first child was born. They reportedly raised 12 children in the area called the Big Woods north and east of Sulphur Springs. John was born in Kentucky and Willie was an orphan raised by various relatives in Louisiana and Arkansas. (Rollins 2002)

Of note is Clyde C. Holley, John Hardin's son, who was born in Delta County and lived on a farm in Hopkins County most of his life. Valton, Clyde's son tells the story about his aunt, Clyde's sister, Opal, who was determined to bring her folks to the Branom Community and get her brother, Clyde a job at the same time. She bought the farm and house on the hill south of the Mt. Zion church and cemetery which became the Holley homeplace.

Clyde worked for a while as a ranch manager and sharecropper, then eventually went to work with the railroad as a brakeman until the war (WWII) came and he was given the choice to go back to farming or get drafted. He went back to farming.

The Holley family just eked out a living on the farm but managed to send most of the girls to college in Commerce. They got teaching certificates and moved away to start lives of their own. Perhaps Valton said it best, "Family farms give way to pasture land and absentee landlords. The kids move away seeking careers in the city. But one thing doesn't change. It's the neighborly spirit of Mt. Zion and the good people who touched our lives as we grew up here." (Rollins 2002)

Clyde married Lucille Nicewarmer and sister, Sybil (Syble) married Ben Herman (Big Ben). There are at least 26 Holley ancestors buried in the Mt. Zion cemetery.

The other HOLLEY family (Clan 2). Originally from Kentucky/Tennessee, W.H. Holley first shows up living in Texas in 1869 in Marion County when he married Lucy Campbell. They apparently never owned land and moved around a lot working mostly as sharecroppers, as was common in those days. Charles Henry (Charlie) married into the McIntire family. Together, they were parents of Charles Thomas and grandparents of Jay Tom Holley.

They lived about a half-mile south of the Charlie Cravens store (intersection of Hwy 11 & Hwy 275) on Highway 275. According to the census, it appears the family lived there during the mid-1930's and into the 1940's, then moved on.

Jay Tom tells a story of how Charlie Cravens helped remove warts from his hand around 1937 by rubbing it. (Rollins 2002)

The SPEED family. 1900 census shows Timothy "Tip" Speed living with his family in Delta County. His son, Elmer S. Speed married into the Vaughn family (old settlers) in 1932, which connected them (Speed family) with many other families in the area who had already intermarried with the Vaughns. Elmer was living in Dallas County when he died, moving on like many who moved after WWII. There are at least 5 Speed ancestors buried in the Mt. Zion cemetery.

The LUNCESFORD family. It appears that Elbridge Gerry Luncesford first settled in Hopkins County and several descendants are buried in the Peerless cemetery. Two of Elbridge's sons lived in the Branom Community: Jasper Kaufman and William Elbridge Luncesford and some of their children attended the Branom school.

As with others, many of the Luncefords have moved on searching for careers in the city. There are at least nine ancestors buried in the Mt. Zion cemetery.

The MILLS family. Originally from Kentucky, John Edward Mills moved his family to Texas sometime around the early 1900's and moved around quite a bit. They moved to the Branom Community in 1939 from a Community north of Sulphur Springs. They bought a 108-acre farm with a three-room house and worked their own crops using the nine children in the family. (Rollins 2002)

Oscar was a congregational Methodist preacher, which probably explained why they continued to move and eventually left the Branom Community. Like many preachers of those days, he attempted to farm and preach to try to support the family.

The FLEENOR family. John Morgan Fleenor of Virginia first appears on the Texas census around 1900. From 1901 and afterwards, his daughters are listed as living near Campbell right on the eastern border in Hunt County, Texas and western border of Hopkins County, near what was once called, 'Westport.'

He had at least 12 children, ten of whom where daughters, so they intermarried with other families in this area. Of note, is Zelma Dee Fleenor, who married Claude Pierce in 1934 and raised their children just down the Cumby highway from Charley Cravens store. They became contributing members of the Community, even though son, Lee Roy Pierce moved away. For example, Lee Roy Pierce has been a long-time trustee for the Mt. Zion Perpetual Care cemetery association and has served up to the ripe old age of 83.

Another Fleenor daughter, Belva Mae Fleenor, married Grover Alton Pipkin, who also lived in the same border area. They also had two sons and several daughters who married into other families in the Hopkins County area. One of their daughters, Elsie Marie Pipkin married William 'Marvin' Haddock, and became **my parents**, making me and my siblings members of the Mt. Zion

199

family.

From the time the Mt. Zion perpetual care cemetery association was formed, records have been kept of who served on the board of trustees and when. Listed below are the families who provided leadership:

1968-69: Stewart family, Carothers family, Burns family, Fitzgerald family, Vaughn family

1970-79: Stewart family, Fitzgerald family, Burns family, Buchanan family, Carpenter family, Butler family, Holley family,

1980-89: Stewart family, Fitzgerald family, Buchanan family, Carpenter family, Holley family, McCool/Gentry family, Speed family, Tucker family.[29]

1990-99: Stewart family, Carothers family, Burns family, Buchanan family, Carpenter family, Holley family, McCool/Gentry family, Speed family, Tucker family, Herman family, Elliott family.

Note: about 1992, Ruth Carothers handed over record keeping to Nita Herman.

2000-2010: Stewart family, Burns family, Buchanan family, Holley family, Speed family, Carothers family, Tucker family, Herman family, Pierce/Fleenor family, Elliott family.[30]

2010-present: Stewart family, Speed family, Carothers family,

---

[29] Neal Stewart served on the board, mostly as President from 1980 to 2018 (present). He represents the longest serving board member and leaves his mark on the present state of affairs of the cemetery.

[30] In 2006, Nita Herman declined the nomination for continuing on the board of trustees.

Tucker family, Herman family, Pierce/Fleenor family, Buchanan family

The Stewart family has had at least one member of the board since its inception. They have also served as officers almost continuously. Presently, there is a third generation Stewart serving on the board who is being groomed to take over. The Carothers family has had representation on the board many times over the years with at least two generations serving. The same is true for the Buchanan family. There is a tradition of being elected to the board and serving until death, unless one resigns. This explains tenure of service on the board spanning around 20 years. One member, a Stewart, has been on the board over 40 years! When one factors in the negative effects of aging, then questions must surface regarding one's effectiveness as a viable leader at some point in time.

Since WWII, people who served the Mt. Zion perpetual care cemetery often had to drive back to the Community to assist and/or attend meetings. This resulted in a board that consisted of people who settled and people who moved away (searchers). This probably added a useful mix of diverse thinking to the board.

Over the years, local people who maintained residence in the Community have come to realize their role to the sustenance of Mt. Zion cemetery. One board member, who lives away, expressed this belief well, "They are plan A, and there is not, nor can there ever be, a plan B. Without them, the cemetery will fall into a state of disrepair. We should appreciate and encourage each and every one of them for whatever efforts they are able to put forth on behalf of the cemetery." This contains much truth, but residents are only *one* of the pillars of the Community and self-sustainability is a narrow focus. Sustainability (not self-sustainability) and renewal is a critical *other* pillar of any Community that must value nonresident input. Nonresidents don't necessarily have to sacrifice an opinion or alternate viewpoint or higher standard to have cooperation from the settlers who stayed. If the cemetery association's demise follows the demise of the Branom Community, County government will probably assume responsibility for caretaking. Either way, rural cemetery associations, must work to make themselves part of an overall plan for renewal and sustainability. This results in a viable plan C with a vision for the future which may have been unseen in prior generations.

When the Baby Boomers were born, they had specific characteristics, and occurred within an observable timeframe, according to some people. World War II ended. You had the post-war rise in standard of living and the rise of the nuclear family. Then societal changes disrupted those patterns, and the generation, for academic purposes, was all over in the mid-sixties.

Baby Boomers -1943-1960

Baby boomers were named for an uptick in the post-WWII birth rate and are often referred to collectively as a 'pig in a python,' symbolizing how they moved through time as a group.

At the end of 1946, the first year of the baby boom, there were approximately 2.4 million baby boomers. In 1964, the last year of the baby boom, there were nearly 72.5 million baby boomers. The population peaked in 1999, with 78.8 million baby boomers, including people who immigrated to the United States and were born between 1946 and 1964.

Bill Clinton was the first baby boomer to serve as president. George W. Bush, Barack Obama and President Donald

Trump are also baby boomers.

According to the Census, the baby boom began in 1946 but demographers Neil Howe and William Strauss, authors of the groundbreaking 1991 book, "Generations: The History of America's Future," argued that the baby boom began as a social and cultural phenomenon with people who were born in 1943.

Baby Boomers can tell you about Woodstock, the Vietnam War, the Beatles, the Civil Rights movement, television, blah, blah, blah. This is my generation. I'm a part of it and we tend to exaggerate our self-importance.

Positives: See above. Also created the Internet, paving the way for the information revolution. Made rock music the dominant cultural influence. Gave us Spielberg, Letterman, Oprah, Ali and Joe Montana.

Negatives: Rewrite history too often to inflate own importance, selfish, doubled the divorce rate of their parents, still obsessed with acting young, even though they're not.

Also, note that the term "the Me Generation" is sometimes applied to Baby Boomers to contrast them with the self-sacrificing Greatest Generation that came before them. ... Members of Generation Me not only want to be wealthy and famous, they feel they deserve it. They went to college, and some of them stayed there.

Generation X – 1961-1981

PROS: Most of the respondents in the study (70%) believed that Gen X are the most effective managers compared to managers from the Boomer (25%) or Gen Y (5%) generation. Members of Gen X scored the highest when it comes to being a "revenue generator" (58% of respondents agree), possessing traits of "adaptability" (49% of respondents agree), "problem-solving" (57% of respondents agree) and "collaboration" (53% of respondents agree).

CONS: Gen X-ers scored the lowest compared to other generations when it comes to displaying executive presence (28%) and being cost effective (34%).

Gen X respondents ranked workplace flexibility as the most important perk (21%) and are more likely to walk away from their current job if flexibility isn't available (38% versus 33% of Gen Y and 25% of Boomers).

By the early 1980's another frontier stage emerged in the nation. If attracted to city work and life, people began to re-think their patterns of living as technologies of the new frontier opened options unavailable until this time. With the inventions of computers and related technologies, people no longer had to travel to the workplace. This meant that people living almost anywhere could receive instantaneous communications from anywhere else and respond to them.

The concept of telecommuting provided a new freedom and new directions.

Consequently, people began to focus either on moving back to their hometowns or to small or mid-sized communities outside urban settlements. Called 'edge cities,' areas such as Pleasant Grove, Garland and Mesquite first expanded to Quinlan, Rowlett, and Rockwall and are still expanding all the way to Royce City and Greenville. Some people call it urban sprawl.

A new concept of space emerged from this frontier

movement: cyberspace, a fourth dimension of space. Cyberspace absorbs conventional space and transforms the land and its use.

As the century ended, a new generation began growing into adulthood, setting the state for new leaders and pushing baby boomers into positions of leadership.

Summary

Significant settler families are: Jetton, McLeroy, Tucker, Swift, Reed, Herman, Fleenor, Pierce, Arrington, Gunter, Boswell, Holley, Buchanan, Speed, Lunceford, Mills, and the many listed who served the cemetery association through the years, whether they remained in the Community or not.

8 THE NEW Century – 2000 to present

Millennials (1982-2004)

Millennials (Born 1982-2004). The generation that is now moving into power in America, with several decades of dominance to come, overlap with the baby boomers. Often criticized as lazy and entitled, but that's usually by baby boomers (who think they're too important) and Gen-Xers (who are whiners).

Pros: Creative thinkers who consider innovation natural. Motivated by relationships and happiness, rather than job security. Accepting of those who are different. Changed how we communicate by embracing and enhancing all forms of new media.

Cons: Still live in their parents' house at 30. Haven't produced a significant political leader (oldest member of generation is just 34, though). Reality TV watchers. Some confusing style choices (in the eyes of a baby boomer). Justin Bieber.

They are sometimes referred to as the Me-Me generation to point toward an excessive focus on themselves. Along the way, this attitude has affected all generations living during this time to a certain degree. An underlying instinct for survival, desire for safety and security, was transformed to a desire to protect the ego. It became a motivation for survival and safety of the ego, the sense of self.

Howe and Strauss introduced the term millennials in 1992, the year their book, "Generations," was published. (Strauss 1992)

In 2014, the number of millennials in the United States eclipsed the number of baby boomers, according to the Census Bureau. The Census counted approximately 83.1 million millennials, compared with 75.4 million baby boomers. Millennials represent one quarter of the nation's population. The Census also reported that millennials are more diverse than previous generations, as 44.2% are part of a minority race or ethnic group.

About 15% of millennials age 25-35 lived at home with their parents as 2016, according to a Pew Research study. Fewer members of older generations lived at home with their parents between the ages of 25-35. The rate for Generation-X was 10%. Baby Boomers ranged between 8% and 11%. The Silent Generation was 8%. Education factored into the percentage of millennials living at home. Among millennials without college degrees, 20% lived at home with their parents.

In a 2016 report, Pew found that young men were more likely to live with a parent than a spouse or domestic partner, with 35% living with parents and 28% living with spouses or partners. It's a reversal from 1960, when about 56% of young men lived with spouses or partners while 23% lived in their parents' homes.

According to a 2015 Census study, earnings for young adults who work full time are about $2,000 less than earnings for young adults in 1980. The analysis also found that millennials are more likely to have a college degree than Gen X-ers did in 1980, yet there are also higher numbers of millennials living in poverty vs. their counterparts in 1980.

2016 was the first year any millennial was eligible to run for president (since the minimum age is 35).

As of 2016, the number of millennials ranged from 75.6

million to 92.7 million.

Generational differences are offered to demonstrate how each generation has different values and leaves its mark on history. Looking forward, differences in the values of generations must be considered in planning for the needs of any Community.

A positive move on the part of the Mt. Zion cemetery association was to open membership and 'stock holder' options for families who were not historically settled in the Community. This option was previously approved and further clarified further in 2017, which provided a process whereby a family name could be presented and eventually approved to sell grave sites to outside families. However, the process has been slow and controlled with very few families, essentially 'adopted.'

New families who have been 'adopted' to the Branom Community or Mt. Zion family probably are retired or near retirement with their children already out of the house. Some examples are listed below:

The other Clinton (clan 2) family. Kenneth L Clinton is a professor emeritus, having taught in sociology and selected in 2015 at TAMU-Commerce. He now owns property in the Branom Community and might be considered as 'adopted' into the Mt. Zion family as his family owns lots in the cemetery and have an ancestor buried there in 2001.

The McFarland family. Keith D. McFarland, is president emeritus of TAMU-Commerce, having served 1998 to 2008. After retirement, he served as acting provost and vice president of academic affairs at Texas Woman's University and interim president at TAMU-Texarkana.

This marks a positive move, that is, marketing to university faculty and staff. The Community is only about four miles from Commerce and could be a destination Community for the homeowner who wants to live outside city limits and away from larger cities. At some point, this could become a goal in revitalization of the Branom Community.

While the initial stages of frontiers traditionally moved from east to west and from rural to urban, the new frontier is multidimensional. Like other frontiers, it still follows the path of least resistance. This will involve removing unnecessary barriers.

With this comes the need to promote political participation in the new frontier in a new century by Millennials and those who follow them as searchers. Someone must study their character of political participation: the mean by which an individual may attain their goals or secure their interests or improve themselves socially and economically. Politicians, like their constituents, judge what is normal or extraordinary by subjective and conditioned (programmed) means. They pay attention to public demand and only commit to supporting what the public wants or invite innovative programs only when they perceive an overwhelming public demand for them to act. (Elazar 2004)

Family dynasties

Family dynasties, like the Medici family, can be traced back in time, mostly after the pattern has been established. For example, we know they first attained wealth and political power in Florence, Italy in the 13th century through its success in commerce and banking. Beginning in 1434 with the rise to power of Cosimo de' Medici, the family's support of the arts and humanities made Florence into the cradle of the Renaissance, a cultural flowering rivaled only by that of ancient Greece. The Medicis produced four popes (Leo X, Clement VII, Pius IV and Leon XI), and their genes have been mixed into many of Europe's royal families. The last Medici ruler died without a male heir in 1737, ending the family dynasty after almost three centuries. Therefore, a sense of survival for a dynasty becomes transposed into a desire for a male heir. This became obvious among the royal families of Europe.

Other contemporary examples, on a national level, are the Bushes, beginning with Prescott Bush, the clan has produced two presidents, two governors, and a host other public servants, and then there are the Clintons…. but they don't have any surviving male heirs that we know about.

From looking at their pattern, it appears that a family dynasty stems from several key ingredients: 1) attaining wealth; 2) rising to power and sharing it with the Community through the arts and humanities, 3) serving others and 4) surviving several generations. Sadly, like royalty, the dynasty ends when no male heir is produced.

21st Century Dynasties

Branom Community has produced no family dynasties on that grand level but do connect to a few families that have shown both staying power and, in some cases, wealth. Some even yielded political power, temporarily.

Staying power, however, may have overly-focused on self-sustainability rather than Community sustainability and renewal.

By the turn of the 20th century, the marriage patterns began to yield connections to the Branom Community that ran roots even deeper into the soil and history. Many descendants, remain locked to the land even to the time of this writing. At this point, each family that still resides in the area will be traced back to their beginnings.

Lytle family

Vernon Lytle married into the pioneering Matthews family 10 Sep 1922. Looking back at the 1872 map, we see two pieces of land owned by the Matthews family, adjoining one plot of land owned by the Box family in that same area referred to as 'Westport' near the Cameron property that was purchased by Clarence Lytle in the 1940s. Therefore, they probably had opportunities to interact with those families over time. When this marriage happened, the Lytles connected back to original settlers such as, not only the Matthews family, but also the Box family.

In addition, when Clarence Jesse Lytle bought the old Cameron place, in the 1940's, he became a fixture in this area that remains to this day. Clarence's children, Beverly LYTLE Pirkey and Clarence Jerry Lytle both live on the land Clarence purchased in the '40's. Besides dairy and cattle farming, the Lytle family supplemented their wealth by working in the field of education. None of the Lytle family have served on the Mt. Zion cemetery board.

Stewart family

William Lawrence Stewart moved into the Branom Community after he lost his wife, Mary Louise Hudson, and relocated from the Celeste area. They had several children together before she passed. On January 19, 1902, he and two daughters transferred their membership to the Mt Zion

Cumberland Presbyterian Church. Another daughter was received by baptism. By April, two sons of the first marriage, followed their father's footsteps. They were Oscar and Fleetwood Stewart and their wives. (Butler 1967) Later that year, sometime in November 1902, he married Mary Elizabeth 'Lizzie' Herman.

The blood connection has been found with this Herman and the other Herman family who still has descendants living in Branom.

W.O. 'Oscar' Stewart. Born in Celeste and moved with his dad to Branom in 1902, he seems to have inherited his religion and followed his dad's footsteps.

W.O. Stewart, Jr., grandson of W.L. Stewart, was made elder of the church on August 31, 1941 and Oscar, Jr.'s son, W.R. 'Raymon' was made Deacon on that same day. Raymon and his wife, Lucille VAUGHN Stewart reared their daughter in the same church. (Butler) 1967)

Raymond's son and daughter, Neal Stewart and Yvonne STEWART Rollins, are still living in the area and have long tenures of service on the board of trustees of the Mt Zion Cemetery Association. Both are now in their 80's. Neal's son lives in the area and serves on the board, making three generations of service.

Herman family

As mentioned, a blood connection has been found with Lizzie Herman and the Ben Herman family who still has descendants living in Branom. It looks like they are all distant relatives of Stephen Isreal Herman whose descendants came from Alabama in the mid-1800's.

Big Ben, aka William Ben Herman, Sr. and his son, Little Ben, operated a dairy and hay farm across the railroad north of the Mt Zion cemetery. Little Ben, aka William Ben Herman, Jr., married Juanita 'Nita' CRAVENS, daughter of Charley and Brooksie VAUGHN Cravens.

Brooksy M. VAUGHN Cravens was from the George Thomas Vaughn and Mattie Pauline STEWART Vaughn family, original settlers in Branom.

It appears their wealth was made in the dairy and hay farming business and supplemented with outside employment, as was the case in this Community for many who stayed.

The Hermans have two generations of service on the board with Nita CRAVENS Herman and her children, two sons and one daughter, serving on the board at various times. Currently, there are no descendants serving.

Tucker family

George Richard Tucker moved to Hopkins County in the Branom area sometime after 1920 where he died. He is buried in the Emblem cemetery. There are only a limited few Tuckers buried in the Mt. Zion cemetery. His son, Harley Tucker and related family lived (and still live) in the Branom Community and are known for their red-haired offspring. The family was in the dairy and cattle ranching business, probably a basis for their wealth. Glendale Tucker first married into the Jetton family. After his wife, Myra, died, he married Katherine Luella "Kathy" Johnson Wagner, a descendant of the Box family. From FAG, we know that her great grandfather, Squire Box, was a founding father in Cumby. Glendale was a member of the Mt. Zion board of trustees for many years and his son, Buff, who lives in the Branom Community, now serves adding two generations of service.

Pierce family

Lee Roy Pierce, born in 1934 (from the Silent Generation), and a descendant of the <u>Frank Pierce family and Fleenor family</u>, is another example of a person who served on the board of trustees of the Mt. Zion perpetual care cemetery association for years (and still serves at this time at 83). Early on, he left the Community for the Dallas/Ft. Worth area, developed a construction business, bought land, and prospered, probably the basis of his wealth. While his sister, Ruth, who lives in the area, served on the board briefly, his son, who lives in the D/FW area, has not shown an interest at this time.

Buchanan family

James Scott Buchanan, a descendant of the pioneering Burns family and one branch that moved away, served as temporary secretary at first. Afterwards James Scott actively provided leadership for the trustees, periodically suggesting the development of a landscaping plan for the cemetery and serving mostly as secretary on the board from 1970 until his death in 2009. The landscape plan was never made, let alone implemented. He served as a trustee for about 39 years, the second longest period of service. He was employed by Austin College in Grayson County. His son, John Scott now serves on the board, even though he lives in the Austin/San Antonio area.

What didn't last

In her little booklet on the History of Mt. Zion, Mrs. Jesse BUTLER Broadfoot (optimistically) stated that with such citizens living and working in the Community, as the descendants of the Boxes, Vaughns, Stewarts, Burns, Camerons, Bouchers, Greaves, she anticipated that the same high-quality leadership that made up old Mt. Zion would continue.

That didn't last.

The Branom public school existed until about 1953 and then were closed, with the building being converted to a Community center. At that time, the schools were consolidated with the Cumby school district, and by the early 1960's, all that remained of the Community was the church and a cemetery.

Those remaining make up a small nucleus of the cemetery board with a few who drive in from other areas. During the late 1980s Mount Zion was a dispersed rural Community and remains this way even today. The area was a thriving farming Community for around 100 years, then dwindled to what remains.

Valton Holley said, "It's the neighborly spirit of Mt. Zion and the good people who touched our lives as we grew up here." (Rollins 2002)

That may have been true then, but the neighborly spirit didn't last. It declined and/or moved away with the people, a decline that began after WWII.

Neither did the pioneer mindset.

Eventually, the Community, itself, didn't last, except in name.

Though not all-inclusive, we know there were over 30 families who were living in Hopkins County during the pioneer days. After families moved out of the Branon Community during and following WWII, there were probably less than 30 families remaining. Broadfoot's (A.S. Broadfoot 1967) historical booklet reflects less awareness of the decline and its effects, but one could consider it implied.

As modern life has become more comfortable, the essential element of the pioneer mindset that has been lost is a sense of responsibility, risk-taking, and work ethic. When one is reduced to valuing consensus over problem-solving and quashing controversy over sorting out truth, there is no room for Community. This just breeds complacency instead of true leadership. There must be a tolerance for the storm before a true Community of diversity can be welcomed in peace with open arms.

History marks WWII as the beginning of the decline of this Community. Along the way, there were signs or markers of the demise of the Branom Community. Yvonne Stewart Rollins mentioned the decline in the introduction of her booklet in 2001. (Rollins 2002) One can even go back to 1953, when the school closed, or 1963 to see markers of decline when the Methodist church in the Branom Community was disbanded. In between those times, the need for a cemetery association, formed in 1968, could be interpreted as another marker of decline in the Community. However, it was overlooked as a marker of decline by many.

Those remaining in the Branom area no longer challenged to function as a Community. They are just a remnant of the past. There is a residual value, and even, pride regarding a lack of conflict. It has been repeated many times and quoted in newspaper articles. This contributes to a form of dysfunction that puts pressure on anyone who has a different point of view and tends to silence whistleblowers when mistakes are made.

What won't last

Trustees have joked that once elected to the board, you serve until you die. When the association was formed, there were no provisions for removing a trustee from the board, even though they had term limits. Over time, as trustees aged past 70, normal cognitive functioning diminished, especially fluid intelligence, manifested by the ability to solve novel problems, plan, and imagine what could be. Past age 80, memory and decision-making become compromised, especially ability to solve complicated unfamiliar problems. Some people age better. Others develop dementia. About 30 percent of people over 80 show symptoms of cognitive decline, not dementia (CIND). Either way, with age and death, decline is inevitable. (S. Karger AG 2008)

Psychological barriers

Well-meaning people are still just people and carry with them their own psychological barriers to aging gracefully. One such barrier is procrastinating, putting things off until it may become a crisis into to get it done in a timely manner. Another is control, trying to say grace over that which is not manageable alone. This can become a problem when aging is threatening one's autonomy, such as keeping the privilege of driving. Ego traps, represent a final barrier when one gets too wrapped up in their sense of self, as opposed to their essential self. If not careful, their reputation is over-valued at the expense of humility.

Well-meaning people continue to serve without acknowledging the stages of life and predictable decline with aging. In our culture, we fall into ego traps such as thinking and believing, 'it (cognitive decline) won't happen to me' and 'if it happens, I'll notice and take action then.' Further, in the last stage of life, beginning around age 72, business, family, secular life, the beauties and hopes of youth and the success of maturity begin to be left behind. Eternity alone remains. And, so it is to *that* - and, not to the tasks and worries of their life, already gone which came

217

and gradually passed like slowly awakening from a dream - that the mind is turned.[31]

At this stage, one has his spiritual eye on goods that men can't give and cares little for anything that men can take away. Therefore, he is beyond the possibility of either seduction or threat. An indirect Biblical reference from martyred missionary Jim Elliot, comes to mind, "He is no fool who gives what he cannot keep, to gain what he cannot lose."[32]

When the cemetery association was set up in 1967, it was called 'perpetual care.' In words, the implication is that the cemetery was setting up a trust fund of money dedicated to the maintenance of the graves perpetually and, if unable to do so, then the courts of the area will see that the provisions of the agreement is carried out.

However, there never was an official trust fund established. It was a savings account whose funds were deposited to draw interest with the interest used to support maintenance. With a decline the cemetery association and its supporters, those funds won't last as interest rates and donations dwindle while leadership deteriorates.

In an environmental context, "sustainability" generally means finding a way to use resources in a manner that prevents their depletion. For charitable nonprofits, the phrase "sustainability" is commonly used to describe a nonprofit that can sustain itself over the long term, perpetuating its ability to fulfill its mission.

---

[31] in Hinduism: the fourth (the ascetic) is like going full circle or completing the circle of life. Source: Mailerindia.com.

[32] "Jim Elliot Quotes," Goodreads.com, accessed November 3, 2017.

Sustainability in the nonprofit context includes the concepts of financial sustainability, as well as leadership succession planning, adaptability, and strategic planning.

Being frugal does not stop consumption, it merely slows it down. One of the challenges of so-called sustainable development: money eventually runs out. To be sustainable, one must do things (like fundraising) in perpetuity or at least for several generations. Consequently, most non-profits walk a fine line between hope and despair.

The message is clear: serving on the board of trustees is <u>not</u> perpetual, neither are the funds. Collectively, there has been little strategic planning and less adaptability making the association unsustainable. If the cemetery association becomes defunct, the cemetery could fall into a state of disrepair and become a perpetual nightmare for local, County, and state officials.

Another message becomes clear: life in a Community has a transient nature. Things, such as frontiers, generations, or even our understanding of time, person, and space (or place), last only for a brief time.

The central problem is how to accommodate newness, population turnover, and the transient nature of life as a *way of life*.

Resolve and preserve

A message for both the settlers and searchers: We cannot "get there"; we can only "be there"—which ironically is to "be here!" Love, like prayer, is not so much an action that we do, but a reality that we are. We don't decide to be loving. When we fall into an ego-threatening style of living that involves a self-centered belief of entitlement and protection of turf, we have lost the love: positive qualities of leadership, neighborliness, and family.

Love is our true and essential self. It is where we came from and where we're going. In short, the Mt. Zion family is at risk of dying off and being forgotten. Like the Community, the love for Mt. Zion is dwindling.

The Mt. Zion cemetery association and the connected church organizations are the primary things that remain in the Community connecting the past, present and future. The church shares two denominations and functions much like a Community church rather than two separate denominations and suffers somewhat from an identity problem. The Mt. Zion cemetery bonds religious denominations together and continues to have a collective identity and board of trustees. Therefore, it is identified as a remnant of the Branom Community that needs saving.

Save, sustainability, preserve – these words do not necessarily mean the same things. The cemetery association may need saving, but in what form? Sustainability is the issue, if it can be saved. But it must be more than self-sustainability. Preservation is an issue that transcends the association itself.

But cemetery preservation presents a unique issue. Cemeteries are, by definition, *lifeless*. The dead buried in cemeteries didn't live there or accomplish their life's work there. A cemetery is, by nature, at a remove (separated, a distance away). On top of that, it's impossible to parse cemeteries from the reason cemeteries exist: *death*. Death is scary, sometimes spooky, and usually sad, and cemeteries are teeming with dead bodies.

Cemeteries are more than the sum of their parts: they are

storybooks. Everyone buried there has a history and a life story that can be brought back to life. Activating that history is a key to both preservation and sustainability. This can be accomplished through genealogical and historical profiles that can be re-created on each person interred there. Once re-created, historical re-enactments can be constructed and offered as part of a cemetery tour. Cemeteries are like museums. Collectively, a cemetery tells the story of a Community. In this sense, a cemetery tour can become a play that tells a story of the settlement in a Community or region, like the play and musical drama at Palo Duro Canyon state park. (palo-duro-canyon n.d.)

A new frontier situation exists

With the technology available, a new frontier exists that provides the ability to re-enact history that makes it come alive, even in a cemetery setting. A frontier situation generates a psychological orientation toward the frontier on the part of the people engaged in conquering it, endowing them with the 'frontier spirit.' There must be room allowed for the return of the seekers on the part of the settlers. With their return, seekers will bring diverse thinking and a comfort with conflict that accompanies problem-solving.

Summary

If you can read this without becoming alarmed or motivated, then your love for the Mt. Zion family may have gone and you may have become complacent beyond help. Similarly, your love for preservation and sustainability of our history may be waning. In the spirit of ending on a positive note, there is hope. The next chapter will provide a summary of the historical and cultural significance of the Mt. Zion Cemetery[33], followed by a chapter about goals and methods for sustainability that all diminishing communities must face.

---

[33] This chapter follows a narrative history that can be used for application of a 'historical' designation by the Texas Historical Commission, if anyone wants to take up this cause.

9 SUMMARY OF MT. ZION CEMETERY AND ITS SIGNIFICANCE

As stated, to understand the geography and lay of the land is to understand it's history.

Following the terrain from Cumby due north as the crow flies, one would pass over the Mt. Zion Cemetery and, eventually, run into the river. Similarly, one cannot delve into the history of an area with running into the importance of cemeteries as a source of basic and precious information.

Overview:

Sumner Bacon, an unofficial Cumberland Presbyterian missionary, arrived in Texas in 1829, making his home in the San Augustine area. (Brackenridge 1968) Bacon preached where he could find worshipers, fought alongside Sam Houston in the revolution, and, in 1833, became an official agent of the American Bible Society. The Cumberland branch of the Presbyterian church was organized in 1810, developing out of a schism during the evangelical revival that opened the century. A Cumberland church was organized in Red River County as early as 1833. (RELIGION IN EARLY TEXAS 2018) However, Bacon is credited as organizing the first Cumberland Presbyterian Church in Texas in the summer of 1836. On September 15, 1838, R. O. Watkins was formally licensed to preach the gospel and was directed to preach on a 'circuit' between the Sabine and Neches Rivers. (Brackenridge 1968)

The Event(s). 1849: The Cumberland Presbyterian Church at Mt Zion, was organized about 1849 by Rev. Anthony Travelstead,

223

a circuit-riding minister out of Paris, with 13 members. The Finley family and their descendants were charter members of this church and intermarried with other pioneer families who settled the area. Many of the early settlers in Red River County and surrounding areas were from Kentucky, Tennessee, and Missouri and of Scots-Irish descent, therefore, had protestant (Presbyterian) roots. In closer proximity to Branom, it was the Finley family who seem to have settled there prior to 1830 and were of Scots-Irish descent and from Missouri. (A.S. Broadfoot 1967)

1850. Chapel Hill College. While the Cumberland Presbyterians were falsely labeled as light on 'book learning,' they did establish Chapel Hill College in Dangerfield, then Titus County prior to the organization of Morris County in 1875.

On January 8, 1849, Allen Urkhart gave land for the college on the condition it be built in Dangerfield. It was located on Highway 259 in Daingerfield near the Presbyterian Church. (T. H. Campbell 2017)

Urquhart gave forty (40) acres of land and pledged one half of the proceeds from the sale of his remaining lots in the original town Plat for the erection of the college buildings.

This male only college, Chapel Hill, operated from 1852 until 1869 when it was closed due to lack of students and finances. (McFarland 2010)

This event probably cemented the connection between this area and Cooper County, Missouri and brought additional families to the area. For example, John Wear (Weir), brother to Hugh Wear and ancestor of Catherine FINLEY Branom and Mary Polly WEAR (WEIR) Burns, served on the first board of trustees.

The Mt. Zion church and cemetery were apparently established together and referred to as Mt. Zion as early as 1850 and they were both associated to the biblical reference, but no other references are available regarding how it got its name. Officially, the church was called the Harmony Presbyterian Church, with the word, 'harmony' meaning unity, concord. On December 24, 1858, David Finley gave two acres on which to build the church home. Ten days later, Nicholas Harlow gave another acre adjoining the first two acres. Both pieces of land were deeded to the Methodist Episcopal and Cumberland Presbyterian churches. This would be the provision of enough land to begin formal burials in a cemetery. In 1901, when a public road (Hwy 11) was planned that would go through church property, additional land was deed to the church and cemetery: Mr. and Mrs. John A. Raines deeded land on the east and Charles E. Brown deeded land on the south. It is believed the present church building was built in 1905. It wasn't until around this time, October 26, 1901, that the name was changed to Mt Zion Cumberland Presbyterian Church. One-half acre of land was donated in 1975 by Lucille Holley and her sons to west side of cemetery. (Rollins 2002) In 2005, 3.088 acres of land on the south and west side of the cemetery was purchased from the Holley family.

By the time the Mt. Zion Perpetual Care Cemetery Association was formed in 1969, most of the families who stayed and settled were related to everyone else, including those who had moved on searching for better opportunities. This happened during a lifetime, but it impacted and overlapped several generations. Many still had childhood memories of a beginning in the Branom Community and how it was.

History does not take place in a vacuum; it is dynamic and interconnected, and the context explores various elements. Oversight of the historical significance of old grave markers highlights only one of the unfortunate results when preservation was overlooked. Cemeteries are money pits, once income from selling lots ceases or dwindles down. The Mt. Zion cemetery is still active with additional land to accommodate another thousand graves and had burials as recent as 2017. However, the cemetery needs to highlight its historical significance to preserve what was, improve what is, and move forward with sustainability into the future.

Historical/Cultural Significance:

The cemetery at Mt. Zion and its adjoining church building are remnants of one of the earliest protestant churches in this part of Texas.

In the early days, it appears that the recorded pioneers, present before the close of 1830, in Texas and the greater Red River County that ended up with descendents in the Hopkins County, Texas area were the Ragsdales and Haddox (alias Coe) families. The Ragsdales married into the Yates family (in Texas by 1834) whose descendants are buried in Mt. Zion, as well as descendants of the Haddox family. Thomas A. Yates fought with Ben Milam in the campaign of Bexar as a volunteer in the Texas revolution. (Haddock, Pillars of Mt. Zion: History of Western Hopkins County and the Branom Community TBA)

Marrying into the Finley family in 1842, was another early settler, Capt. Merit Branom. Merit B. Branom is one of the best-known pioneers who settled Hopkins County (still Lamar County then) in the Emblem Community and had the Branom Community named after him. He was born in the State of Missouri about 1820 and moved to this County about 1839 or 1840. He was reported to be of Catholic faith and French ancestry, therefore, didn't join the protestant (Presbyterian) church right away, but later became a member along with his children. The first authorized settlers in Texas had to swear preferences for the Catholic church, since Mexico was predominately Catholic. Together, Merit Branom and his wife, Ellen FINLEY, both from Missouri, had 14 children in 20 years, leaving descendants to intermarry with other pioneer families. The Finley family intermarried with the Wear (Weir) family in Missouri, who were prominent in the Cumberland Presbyterian Church. Mary Polly Wear married Laird Burns a Cumberland Presbyterian minister who eventually settled in the Mt. Zion area with his family.

What circumstances in the area helped lead to the event?

Just as immigration to America substantially increased with the introduction of the Headright System in 1691, Texas attracted settlers by offering incentives for settling in the area. This idea of granting land to settlers as an incentive that came from the Romans and was carried over all the way to other states as they were being settled.

Texas was settled from the east to the west by people who primarily came from the United States seeking land and prosperity. All those who came to the old Red River District (in Texas) before the close of the year 1830 moved into foreign territory, even paid taxes in two countries during a time of disputed ownership and participated in governmental affairs during early Texas history. (Ed H. McCuistion, October, 1995)

Some are obvious, as they played an active role in helping

Texas obtain its independence. Ben Milam, who led the campaign of Bexar and died there, fought with Thomas Yates. His role was obvious. He was buried in San Antonio where he died and it appears his relatives stayed mostly in other states in the south. Others were more obscure, like the Yates family who received no glory and the Finley family, and simply came to establish their familes in the area. At least four Finley descendants are buried in the Mt. Zion cemetery, along with Yates descendants.

Of special interest, there is a concrete tomb located above ground in the Mt. Zion cemetery that seldom goes unnoticed but has little documentation. There is at least one story about it and this artifact requires more research. Scarce experimental data exists describing postmortem effects of burial in cement. (Haddock, Pillars of Mt. Zion: History of Western Hopkins County and the Branom Community TBA)

At least one descendant in the Mt. Zion cemetery, from the Box family, had ancestors who: 1) were massacred by the Comanches after the Civil War and 2) other ancestors who converted to the Mormon church in the 1850's and moved to Utah.

How does the event relate to the history of its Community, County, region?

Settlement in western Hopkins County was a part of the first phase of rural frontier settlement that went from east to west and, in Texas, from the wooded to the plains regions.

Early settlers and their descendants held important positions of governmental leadership, such as County offices, state representatives, and, even national positions. As they intermarried, descendants of the Finley family connected with many of the early leaders of western Hopkins County. For example, Merit Branom, an early settler, Texas Ranger, and Civil War officer, had a son, <u>William J. 'Bill' Branom</u> who was sheriff of Hopkins County for 6 years. Dave Finley, a descendant of the Finley family, was a County tax assessor. Also, they became landowners and contributed to the tax base of Hopkins County. For example, <u>G. W. Halbrook</u> – Was the son of Katherine FINLEY Halbrook and John Melton Halbrook. A Daniel Halbrook(s) owned several large tracts of land along the South Sulphur border in the Branom Community, according to the old 1872 map. Also, a <u>H.J. Halbrook</u> was listed as obtaining an early liquor license in Cumby. Richard C. 'Uncle Dick' Carpenter was an old settler of Hopkins County and left descendants who are buried in the Mt. Zion cemetery. He was 88 years old when he died, a native of IRELAND, having come to the United States when a young man. He enlisted in the Confederate Army in the state of Virginia and came to Hopkins County about the year of 1868 and continued to make this County his home thereafter. He may be one of the most honored Civil War soldiers in the County. He served four terms as commissioner of Hopkins County and one term as superintendent of the County farm. He had at least one descendant who also served as a County commissioner and ran a store in the Branom Community. (Haddock, Pillars of Mt. Zion: History of Western Hopkins County and the Branom Community TBA)

The Cumberland Presbyterian church didn't divide (into north and south branches) in the Civil War, like the Presbyterian Church did. In 1906, when other Cumberland Churches united with the Presbyterian Church (USA), Mt. Zion church didn't. The headquarters of the denomination is in Memphis, Tennessee centered in the Memphis Theological Seminary. In Texas, a college that was started by the Cumberland Presbyterian Church is Trinity

University in San Antonio. (Rollins 2002) Founded in 1869, and leaving a unique history on the region, Trinity University has resided on four campuses in three separate locations[34].

What is its relevance to the broader history?

While the overall settlement of the Branom Community, its church and cemetery, is an important piece of history of this part of the County, its eventual decline has been overlooked by historians and local citizens, as the area has progressed through several phases of modern frontier life. Currently, that history of that time and place is in danger of being lost completely if not supported by historic preservation groups. A specific example is the preservation of historic grave markers. One example of a remedy: in an historic North Carolina cemetery, they built a wall in an older part of it showing the missing graves of pioneers and details that were preserved from the old, broken markers that are missing.

Cemeteries are more than the sum of their parts: they are storybooks. Everyone buried there has a history and a life story that can be brought back to life. Activating that history is a key to both preservation and sustainability. This can be accomplished through genealogical and historical profiles that can be re-created on each person interred there. [see bio sketch on Laird Burns & Harvey McClinton in Documentation] Once re-created, historical re-enactments can be constructed and offered as part of a cemetery tour. Cemeteries are like museums. Collectively, a cemetery tells the story of a Community. In this sense, a cemetery tour can become a play that tells a story of the settlement in a

---

[34] Tehuacana (1869-1902), Waxahachie (1902-1942), and San Antonio (1942-present)

Community or region, like the play and musical drama at Palo Duro Canyon state park. (palo-duro-canyon n.d.)

What other events took place that may have had a bearing on how or why the event was important?

Everyone buried in the cemetery connects to a larger family, some of whom were pioneers in other places in Texas. Many family stories can be traced to broader histories of the state and nation.

The decline of the rural frontier was unmonitored by policy makers, politicians and local citizens as opportunities resurfaced with continued emergence of modern frontiers. For example, with the cyberspace frontier, came new opportunities for rural communities that have not been fully explored. Additionally, the use, preservation and dissemination of historical information has become more relevant and accessible with internet and computer technology applications to genealogical information and historical websites.

The cemetery is conveniently located by Highway 11 West, about 4 miles east of Commerce. There are 795+ graves including the unknowns. It has been maintained through the years but has no significant landscaping or landscaping plan.

Laird Burns is the earliest marked grave in the Mt Zion Cemetery (January 1858, same year land was donated to the church, that December). He was one of the first graduates of the, then, home-based Cumberland Presbyterian Seminary in Missouri, thought to be the first theological school west of the Mississippi. He was married to Mary Polly Wear, daughter of Hugh Wear, an organizing member of the church. **Hugh Wear was from Kentucky and lived in the Ellis neighborhood. He was the father of the Rev.**

Wm. Bennett Wear, another Cumberland Presbyterian of considerable distinction. Laird Burns was an Elder in the McGee Presbytery, considered the mother presbytery of the Cumberland Presbyterian Church in Missouri and one of the first ministers to be ordained in their second meeting held the second Tuesday in September 1820. (Cordry 1976) He had two sons who helped establish a Cumberland Presbyterian Church in Miller Grove.[35]

Robert 'Harvey' McClinton. It is <u>not</u> known that he served as pastor at Mt. Zion, be we know he was ordained as a Cumberland Presbyterian clergyman while still living in Arkansas in 1859. (Wilson 1859) He was from Hempstead, Arkansas (just northeast of Texarkana) and married Syntha Jane BAIRD (a family with a long line of Presbyterians). They both came from families that were considered of Scots-Irish descent. They had family living in Titus and Hopkins County before he moved to Branom with his wife (at least by 1859). Harvey died on November 25, 1865 in Hopkins County and is buried in the Mt Zion Cemetery, Southwest section, Row 1, Gravesite 5. His marker was a flat limestone slab that has been knocked down and broken into several pieces. A small stone identifying his grave has recently been placed to mark his gravesite.

As with Cumby and other cemeteries with historical significance, many of the early grave markers were made from limestone and were easily broken, and later discarded, lost or thrown away. Therefore, some graves are unmarked and lost. Broken grave markers have been discarded, removed from the

---

[35] The Cumberland Presbyterian Church was progressive admitting traditional minorities, such as women and people of color, into church leadership earlier than most.

cemetery and given away. Many were children or markers of early pioneers. Recently (2017) an updated census of people buried in Mt. Zion has been made available online at mtzionhopkins.com and updated simultaneously on Find-A-Grave.com. It was during this time that the removal of broken grave markers was discovered. Other historically significant people buried there includes several Civil War veterans and veterans of other wars. Our country owes its life to heroes whose names it will never know, if not actively preserved. Laird Burns and his wife's graves are marked with a small replacement marker.

In **1999**, the cemetery board authorized the purchase of 34 new grave markers to replace old, broken monuments. Little is known about the degree of follow up and it is uncertain that preservation was a concern, because an ancestor of the Finley family's grave is now marked by a small stone that only lists his name. These small markers have been used to replace the original, but the broken and discarded limestone markers that contained more details were discarded. Those old markers have been victim of cemetery caretakers and their lawn mowers and heavy equipment, such as grave digging machines and dump trucks that have been allowed unsupervised access to the cemetery in recent years. Grave sites that are closet to the cemetery access roads are particularly prone to become victims.

Because they are small, the replaced markers are also prone to sink into the soil and disappear. Collectively, these practices result in much of the historical information of any cemetery to disappear.

Through the progressing decline in the Community, a rural frontier has followed the flight to the city, urban sprawl, and eventually the cyberspace frontier. That new frontier brought a new dimension of space (cyberspace) and offers opportunities for rural locations again, especially those located in close proximately to college towns and communities concerned with quality of life.

10 STRATEGIES for sustainability

In the preface, contemporary issues regarding the quality of life in communities were introduced. Three are re-visited below:

- o Philanthropy and Volunteerism – using incidence of volunteering/giving

- o Neighborliness – using percent comfortable asking a neighbor for help/favor

- o Civic Engagement – using percent voting in local elections by registered voters

While these measures surfaced in recent history, they collectively represent the human desire for a sense of safety and security and have provided an umbrella of concerns for communities to consider. Think through the history of the Branom Community and consider how well this Community has rated through the years, in its pioneer years, its glory years and its declining years. As time has passed, these indicators not only point to a measure of *quality of life*, but also have been used to measure *sustainability* of a Community.

Revisit quality of life

Why? These issues relate to the sustainability of a Community and must be addressed for leaders to measure growth or decline, as well as prepare for the needs of future citizens.

In a climate of domestic terrorism, school shootings, and decline in our institutions of social control, all communities have a growing concern about quality of life indicators and sustainability.

These are the underlying pillars of any Community and are essential to a Community's sustainability. Like any job, the description is the *what*, while the people are the *how*. For any Community to thrive, there must be support for diversity: of people, viewpoints, and values.

Citizens and policymakers often fail to realize gaps in their current information and may not always be collecting what we most need to know to meet our goals in the twenty-first century! Many times, data is collected because "we have always collected it" or because it is easy to collect as a by-product of an ongoing government program. In the case of rural communities, like Branom, it's possible that no one was monitoring the quality of life information as the area was allowed to decline.

In a brief review of sustainability indicators, three U.S. cities identify the following concerns with a slightly different focus on quality of life:

• While stressing the importance of interpersonal relationships to actual feelings about quality of life one city primarily concentrates on the *external environment*.

• Another city *asks several questions*: "How do we protect our environment, meet everyone's basic needs, keep our economy dynamic, and maintain a just society? How do we make difficult trade-offs and balanced judgments that take everyone's interests into account, including those of our children and grandchildren?"

• Still another city focuses on *sustainability as the guiding principle* while acknowledging the importance of quality of life. They state their goal as "recognizing the interdependence of the environment, economic development, and social equity...with a decision-making climate that invests in what is good for today without compromising the future for our children, a climate that benefits each person and the common good."

These different viewpoints highlight the unique values of each Community, meaning that citizens must define the indicators in terms of their collective values. Traditional measures are not enough. They must be defined in terms of sustainability measures for now and the future.

For example, quality of life is just not about economics and availability of goods and services. But there are two important ways in which quality of life measures generally go further than extending the idea of consumption beyond the private sector to public goods.

First, we need a set of measures that extend into the social realm by attempting to measure the quality of relationships between members of the Community and the larger Community. General societal examples are the many indicators of racial relations, of child abuse or family violence and of neighborliness. In the Branom Community, this could involve measuring the relationship between the Community and the University Community in Commerce. These reflect concerns with human relationships as well as with consumption of goods and services.

Another set of indicators measure access to cultural resources, nature, and recreation and civic participation, based on concern with opportunities for personal development in a Community. A university-based city offers greater access to these opportunities and makes proximity to a college town both desirable and attractive to incoming residents.

College towns, for example, are highly favored locations in

the new frontier, linked by their connections in cyberspace. While each frontier has generated its own new world with new opportunities, new patterns of settlement, and new occupations, each also presented new challenges and unfamiliar problems.

Overall experience of life

In general, the focus on the overall assessment of one's life, can be measured using three sub-dimensions:

- life satisfaction (cognitive appreciation), consciously believing you are satisfied with where you live;

- affect (a person's feelings or emotional states, both positive and negative, typically measured with reference to a particular point in time), feeling good about where you live; and

- a sense of having meaning and purpose in one's life, or good psychological functioning, knowing that you are making a difference to the Community in which you live.

Smart growth strategies

Smart growth strategies can help rural communities achieve their goals for growth and development while maintaining their distinctive rural character.

Below are some specific suggestions and local examples:

- Goal: help existing places thrive by taking care of investments and assets

Policy: Planning where development should or should not go can help a rural Community encourage growth in nearby towns, where businesses can thrive on a walkable main street and families can live close to their daily destinations.

- A specific suggestion for the cemetery association, a remnant of organization in the Branom Community, would be to encourage attendance and measure voting practices of people in attendance at the general meetings and board meetings of the association. Do this by linking and networking with planning and development groups in city, educational and County government.

- Goal: support the rural landscape by keeping working lands viable, conserving natural lands and preserving historical landmarks;

  Policy: protect the rural landscape help preserve open space, protect air and water quality, provide places for recreation, and create tourist attractions that bring investments into the local economy.

- A specific suggestion for the cemetery association would be to plan, design and implement a landscaping task group for the gravesites in the cemetery, including preservation of old historical markers, implementing a scatter garden[36], working with local historical organizations.

- Goal: create great new places by building lively and enduring neighborhoods where people want to live.

---

[36] *designated places where the family and friends of the deceased can scatter the cremains of their loved one.*

Policy: support walking, biking, and public transit help reduce air pollution from vehicles while saving people money.

- A specific suggestion for the cemetery association would be re-create the church and cemetery property to be a more inviting destination by considering public access to water, picnic facilities, vending machines and/or parking for travelers. An example would be the County park system in Harris County. Another example, would be the parks and recreation systems in many cities that also operate city cemeteries.

Think of cemeteries as first public parks in America. They enticed residents into an idyllic pastoral experience with rolling green hills, shady trees and stone benches designed for reflective thought. But it wasn't a complete escape. A Community's character is echoed in the landscape of its cemeteries

Often, it's the oldest intact property in town.

More than a burying yard, cemeteries preserve art, like poetry and archaic expressions, on its grave markers. It's not replaceable. It should really be viewed as a museum, although it's in an outdoor environment, and it needs to be taken care of that way.

Since strategic planning has <u>not</u> been done in the Branom Community, an example of one Community's work is provided next.

Example: Action Plan

Though a workshop near El Paso in west Texas, largely

focused in on starting a farmer's market and Community garden, we can see how details are worked into a plan that helps address sustainability issues.

Workshop participants identified several action steps for achieving each goal. The goals and corresponding actions are outlined in this section. The goals and action items are presented in Appendix A in their complete form, which includes a time frame, lead role, supporting cast, cost, funding sources, and near-term steps.

Goal 1: Start a farmers market/Community market to provide a venue for local farmers to sell their produce and for residents to have access to healthy foods.

- Action 1.1 Define the mission and values for the market

- Action 1.2 Identify parameters or requirements for vendors at the market

- Action 1.3 Develop event calendar that the market will coordinate with

- Action 1.4 Identify strong partner to help sustain market – maybe La Fe clinic

- Action 1.5 Identify potential vendors willing to sell at the market

Goal 2: Start a Community garden for the residents that is a place where people can learn, socialize, and grow their own food.

- Action 2.1 Generate and determine interest of Community in having a Community garden by holding a meeting or having an information table at a local event

• Action 2.2 Form a Community garden committee and use volunteer time to help move it forward and serve as a sounding board for identifying sites for the garden, securing the site, and how to use the site

• Action 2.3 Identify site (or sites) for Community garden (consider Dr. Applegate's property)

• Action 2.4 Find other partners for use of site and buildings

• Action 2.5 Secure use of the Community garden site or sites

• Action 2.6 Develop Master Plan and site prep for the garden

• Action 2.7 Identify and recruit growers and people interested in having plots at Community garden

Goal 3: Create a Small Business Incubator to support residents wishing to start their own business by providing them resources and tools necessary for success.

• Action 3.1 Begin communications and outreach to let residents know about existing small business resources; start small business start-up classes or workshops in Vinton

• Action 3.2 Outreach and recruitment of small businesses or potential new businesses.

• Action 3.3 Hire an intake person

• Action 3.4 Conduct longer term needs assessment for space

Goal 4: Start a local foods education program to educate residents on the benefits of eating healthy, locally grown food, and to teach them how to grow their own food.

- Action 4.1 Establish a farmer-to-farmer training program

- Action 4.2 Conduct local healthy eating and active living events

- Action 4.3 Create a backyard gardening program

- Action 4.4 Create a "hands on" green club

- Action 4.5 Develop an internship/apprenticeship program where students are paired with a farmer and work with them over summer break

Implementation ideas

During the workshop, there were discussions of prioritizing goals and which action steps to take first. Some thought the Community garden needed to be started first before beginning the farmers market. At the end of these discussions there was not consistent agreement on which to focus on first.

Conclusion: There is no definitive order that these initiatives are typically implemented in other places; it depends on the unique, individual communities.

Creating a farmer's market that attracts people from all over the region and out of state will positively affect the local economy. Strengthening the local demand for local foods can help foster growth of small farmers and food entrepreneurs. Developing a small business incubator program will support existing small businesses and those starting up.

The actions in this plan will help to support a Community that has been in existence for hundreds of years. The actions focus on supporting local entrepreneurs, and teaching residents how to grow their own food to create a local food system so they can rely less on resources outside of the Community.

A workshop brings together people from many state and federal agencies. The new relationships formed both within Community leadership and with people outside of the Community can attract additional resources to support implementation of this action plan. It is important to nurture these new relationships by finding ways to stay engaged with each other.

Additionally, the workshop efforts identified several opportunities and resources to tap into and leverage different local, state and federal funding sources to support the Community garden, farmers market, education programs, and business assistance.

First, people must organize. Projects, such as this, cannot be done by a few, in most cases. Next, funding must be secured. National, state, and local government entities must be involved to assist, like the USDA, Office of Rural Development.

Example: City of Austin, Texas Cemetery master plan

Background. In Summer, 2013, the steering committee engaged the Community in the development of a scope of work for the Cemetery Master Plan. In September 2013, the steering committee issued a Request for Proposals for a Cemetery Master Plan, including a comprehensive tree survey, for all five City of Austin cemeteries. On February 27, 2014, the Austin City Council authorized the award, negotiation, and execution of a contract with a private company to provide cemetery consulting services in an amount not to exceed $207,647.57. In Spring 2014, the committee began the Cemetery Master Plan process to develop a master plan for Austin's five municipal cemeteries. It was approved in September 2015.

As one can see, this is a multi-year project that involves a steering committee and the organization of an existing governmental entity. In today's climate, governmental support and funding is necessary for any group whose ambition is to be 'perpetual.'

Groups consisting of individuals interested in saving and preserving cemeteries are good starting places to fuel any steering committee.

Who Saves Cemeteries?

Demographics can span from university students to the recently retired. "It's not just, 'Oh, I'm 60 so I better start thinking about cemeteries now' kind of people," says a board member in a Saving Our Cemetery (SOC) organization. If anything, these volunteers think about cemeteries for reasons that have nothing to do with their own mortality. Common denominators run through the group:

- Native citizens with ancestors buried in the area, like a photo documenting volunteer who is both a teacher and rancher;

- Native citizens with ancestors buried in the area who also are professional historians, like a certified archivist, or a genealogist;

- Area transplants with training in archaeology, and architecture;

- Aspiring anthropologists like college students and/or recent graduates;

- Educators who hobby in history, who may operate tours in their spare time, or a high school science teacher, graduate student, and bartender, who may make themselves available as a lecturer; or

- Volunteer-work junkies / tireless do-gooders, who have an interest in old cemeteries while involved in other volunteer activities.

What do communities owe to their dead? How should communities approach historic cemeteries in the 21st century, when citizens are more mobile than ever before? Fewer families remain near the land where their parents, grandparents and great-grandparents are buried. Cremation has become popular, with ashes scattered far beyond the local cemetery. Do communities want their history scattered, like ashes?

Cremation is becoming an increasingly common end-of-life choice. Thanks to a breadth of factors - from increased religious acceptance to burial space considerations – the practice has nearly doubled in popularity over the past several years. As more people have chosen cremation, a variety of options for handling the ashes have increased in popularity to accompany the practice. One of these options is scatter gardens.

Scatter gardens are designated places where the family and friends of the deceased can scatter the cremains of their loved one. These gardens are often beautiful spots. They're picturesque and peaceful areas tended to by a cemetery, designed to offer a beautiful final resting place for those whose ashes are spread there.

Why a Scatter Garden?

For those who choose cremation, there are several benefits to having ashes placed in a scatter garden.

First, a scatter garden makes the process of dispersing ashes as easy and simple as possible for the loved ones of the deceased. While the idea of scattering ashes in a public area may sound nice, there are actually a variety of laws to consider when doing so. In many public areas, scattering cremains is illegal.

Choosing a scatter garden means that family members and loved ones will not have to consider these issues during their time of grief. Instead, they'll be able to feel peace, as the process is made easy for them and they aren't forced to deal with questions of legality. A cemetery can put these issues to rest.

Additionally, scatter gardens provide an option that is more environmentally friendly than scattering at other sites. While there are public and private sites that do legally allow for the scattering of ashes, cremains can have a negative impact on the environment. That's because they commonly contain mercury and dioxins.

At a scatter garden, however, the plot of land where ashes are scattered is carefully maintained so that the environmental impact of the cremains is mitigated.

Finally, choosing a scatter garden can lend a sense of closure to loved ones of the deceased. Some people may find that cremation doesn't give them the traditional sense of connection and closure that traditional burial methods provide. If ashes are scattered in air or water, for example, there is often no place for loved ones to come to remember the deceased.

Dispersing at a scatter garden allows family and friends to have a sense of closure, and gives them a place to return to in order to remember and celebrate their loved one. This is often enhanced by memorial options at scatter gardens, such as plaques, engravings, or benches that offer remembrances of the people resting there. (Good 2016)

Mary Reynolds, an internationally recognized landscape architect, is quoted as saying,

"We are drawn to certain locations where the land resonates with us and pulls us towards it. People can spend their entire lives looking for the places where they belong, places where they feel at home, where they fit and can comfortably set down roots." (Otis Chandler 2018)

As a lover of all things wild and free, I believe in the power of place; that there is one particular place; one particular landscape that exists in which we are most able to feel the restorative power and voice that can only come from connecting to that from which we evolved. For some people, this can be only one place, such as a homeplace. For others, it can be many places and feel like a safe place or even a sacred place. (Haddock, Wounded Healer 2011)

A cemetery landscape plan (that incorporates the use of scatter gardens in areas where grave markers and specific locations of graves have been lost) can be dedicated to a multi-use section that both preserves and protects. For example, Mary Reynolds' award-winning work below provides an illustration of the possibilities (photo taken from internet):

Caretaking of historic cemeteries is important for its own sake, but it is also an elegant way to invest in public parks and public health, to enhance tourism and quality of life, to make communities more sustainable and to knit together a disparate citizenship — all at once. Turning the mundane into transformational change, after all, is the secret of visionaries and pioneers alike.

It is well worth remembering the epitaph on Thomas Yates' grave marker:

"Remember young man as you pass by,

That as you are now, so once was I,

But as I am, so you must be,

Therefore, prepare to follow me."

Billy D Haddock

Appendix A - list of families & classification:

- PATHFINDERS – before the close of 1830
- PIONEERS – 1831- 1850
- OLD SETTLERS – 1851-1870
- SETTLERS – 1870 up to World War II

1. ALEXANDER ... Pioneer family

2. Arnold ... Old Settler Family

3. Arrington ... Settler family

4. Babb ... Pioneer family

5. Beadles ... Settler family

6. Berry ... Settler family

7. Bingham ... Pioneer family

8. Binion ... Settler family

9. Boucher ... Old Settler family

10. Box ... Pioneer family

11. Branom ... Pioneer family

12. Broyles/Broiles Settler family

13. Brown ... Settler family

14. Bulls ... Settler family

15. Burns   ...   Pioneer family

16. Burke   ...   Old Settler family

17. Butler   ...   Old Settler family

18. Cameron   ...   Old Settler family

19. Campbell   ...   Pioneer family

20. Cate   ...   Pioneer family

21. Carothers   ...   Settlers family

22. Carpenter   ...   Old Settler family

23. Clark   ...   Settler family

24. Clinton   ...   Settler family

25. Cravens   ...   Settler family

26. Curlee   ...   Settler family

27. Currin   ...   Old Settler family

28. Davis   ...   Settler family

29. Deakins   ...   Settler family

30. DeSpain   ...   Pioneer family

31. Dorris   ...   Old Settler family

32. Ewing   ...   Pioneer family

33. Fallis   ...   Settler family

34. Finley   ...   Pathfinder family

35. Fleenor   ...   Settler family

36. Garoutte   ...   Pioneer family

37. Garrett   ...   Pioneer family

38. Gentry   ...   Settler family

39. Gillis   ...   Settler family

40. Greaves   ...   Pioneer family

41. Green   ...   Pioneer family

42. Haddock   ...   Settler family

43. Haddox   ...   Pathfinder/Settler family

44. Halbrook   ...   Old Settler family

45. Hammonds   ...   Settler family

46. Harris   ...   Old Settler family

47. Harlow   ...   Pioneer family

48. Herman   ...   Old Settler family

49. Holley -Clan 2 ...   Settler family

50. Holley -Clan 1 ...   Settler family

51. Jackson   ...   Old Settler family

52. Jetton   ...   Settler family

53. Jordan   ...   Pioneer family

54. Kincaid   ...   Old Settler family

55. Kootnz   ...   Pioneer family

56. Ladd   ...   Settler family

57. Lindley   ...   Pioneer family

58. Low(e)   ...   Old Settler family

59. Lunceford   ...   Settler family

60. Lytle   ...   Settler family

61. Maloy   ...   Old Settler family

62. Marrs   ...   Pioneer family

63. Matthews   ...   Pioneer family

64. McAnally   ...   Old Settler family

65. McClinton   ...   Old Settler family

66. McCurdy   ...   Settler family

67. McDonald   ...   Pioneer family

68. McFarlin   ...   Old Settler family

69. McGregor   ...   Settler family

70. McIntire   ...   Old Settler family

71. McManus   ...   Settler family

72. Milam   ...   Pathfinder family

73. Miller   ...   Pioneer family

74. Mills   ...   Settler family

75. Moore(s)   ...   Old Settler family

76. Moreland   ...   Old Settler family

77. Pierce   ...   Settler family

78. Patrick   ...   Settler family

79. Pipkin   ...   Old Settler family

80. Plunkett   ...   Old Settler family

81. Prim   ...   Old Settler family

82. Ragsdale   ...   Pathfinder family

83. Raines   ...   Old settler family

84. Reed   ...   Settler family

85. Riley   ...   Old Settler family

86. Ritchey   ...   Pioneer family

87. Roan   ...   Settler family

88. Rucker   ...   Pioneer family

89. Shelton   ...   Pioneer family

90. Sloan   ...   Settler family

91. Smith   ...   Old Settler family

92. Speed   ...   Settler family

93. Stewart   ...   Settler family

94. Swift   ...   Settler family

95. Taliaferro   ...   Pioneer family

96. Tarrant   ...   Pioneer family

97. Taylor   ...   Settler family

98. Teer   ...   Settler family

99. Tucker   ...   Settler family

100.   Turley   ...   Old Settler family

101.   Vaughn   ...   Old Settler family

102.   Wall   ...   Settler family

103.   Walling   ...   Settler family

104.   Ward   ...   Old Settler family

105.   Wiggs   ...   Old Settler family

106.   Winnifred...   Pioneer family

107.   Wren   ...   Pioneer family

108.   Yates   ...   Pioneer family

109.   Young   ...   Pioneer family

Appendix B – Burials: Mt. Zion 1858-1901

Recorded deaths and burials in Mt. Zion Cemetery from 1858 to 1901. Use this list to identify other descendants who lived and died in the Branom Community. Maiden names of women are in all caps. Note how the families intermarried. To view the complete list, go to: www.mtzionhopkins.com and click on 'database of burials.'

Sec	Row	Lot	LastName	FirstName	Death	Birth
SW	4	11	Burns, Jr.	Rev Lard Lindsey	01/1858	01/1784
SW	4	12	Burns	Mary Polly WEIR	01/1861	01/1792
SW	4	13	Burns	Rufus Godwin	01/1864	06/1856
SW	1	5	McClinton, Rev.	Robert 'Harvey'	11/1865	01/1819
SW	3	13	Ladd	J F (John Fendall)	01/1872	01/1824
SE	9	1	Duncan	Elizabeth Catherine KOONTZ	07/1872	07/1824
SW	9	7	Mangum	Frances Permilia WARD	02/1874	12/1843

SW	9	9	Pickard	Fanny E	11/1874	10/1874
SW	9	4	Ward	Malinda MOORE	01/1878	05/1818
SW	4	9	Burns, Rev	John Perry W	01/1879	01/1819
SE	4	6	Hawkins	Addie	01/1879	01/1879
SW	10	4	Ward	Willie L	06/1880	10/1878
SW	4	20	McAnally	Amanda Ruth SHORES[37]	10/1880	08/1841
SE	5	7	Teer	James Wiley	06/1881	03/1874
SE	5	2	Finley	Viola Lee	09/1881	10/1878
SW	1	3	Moreland	Jimmie	11/1881	10/1880
SE	5	3	Finley	Infant	11/1881	08/1880

---

[37]

10/23/1880 @39	Amanda Ruth SHORES McAnally – was the daughter of Wiley Edward and Ida Frances Shores and wife of <u>William Franklin McAnally</u>.

SW	1	2	Moreland	William	11/1881	02/1852
SE	6	2	Patrick	Mary Ann	11/1881	02/1857
SW	5	4	Greaves	Robert C Smith	01/1882	07/1817
SE	6	3	Patrick	Deby Ann Lucretia DALRYMPLE	01/1882	02/1836
SE	6	1	Patrick	Nancy Ann	01/1882	09/1862
SW	3	12	Ladd	Margaret BURKE	03/01/1882	06/01/1832
SE	5	4	Finley	Infant Son	06/1882	06/1882
SW	1	1	McClinton	Oscar Albert	09/1882	01/1859
SW	4	10	Burns	Lucenda Jane BURKE	01/1883	01/1822
SE	7	13	Burns	Leona Malvina WILLIAMS	01/1883	10/1835
NE	4	21	McGregor[38]	Joseph	09/1883	05/1842

---

[38] 9/15/1883@ 41   Joseph McGregor – was the husband of Lucinda BLOUNT McGregor.

SW	4	3	Burns	Infant	04/1884	03/1884
SE	5	12	Miller	James F	08/1884	11/1882
SW	6	3	Cameron	Ewing	08/1884	08/1882
SW	6	15	Burns	Allen K	03/1885	02/1851
SW	3	20B	Clark	Jimmie	09/1886	09/1886
SW	3	20	Clark	Johnie	09/1886	09/1886
SW	3	16	Vaughn	George C	11/1887	08/1886
SE	7	3	Vaughn	Sarrah Jane MAULTSBY	12/1887	07/1837
SE	9	11	Jackson	Prof Thomas Joseph	01/1888	01/1811
SW	2	4	Wiggs	R A	01/1888	01/1861
SW	3	7	Rash	Infant Son	01/1888	01/1888
SW	3	6	Rash	Mattie Bazoria WALLING	01/1888	09/1868
SW	4	8	Burns	Samuel Jackson	01/1888	10/1826
SW	4	2	Burns	Jimmie	02/1888	12/1882
SW	3	3	Walling	Crockett	03/1888	03/1834

				Hubbard		
SW	11	19	Vaughn	W C Davis	04/1888	12/1849
NE	7	28	Lawrence	George Walton	06/1888	09/1884
SE	7	2	Vaughn	Perry Davis	06/1888	11/1861
SE	5	8	Teer	Flora Celeste	04/1889	11/1888
SE	7	1	Vaughn	Rachel Lucretia PATRICK	10/1889	07/1860
SW	7	4	Moore	Cleopatra P Patria CAVEND	01/1890	01/1849
SW	3	2	Walling	Winnie	07/1890	08/1833
SW	5	2	Burns	Bertie May	02/1891	12/1888
NE	6	21	Glenn	Joseph H	09/1891	08/1889
SW	3	8	Rash	Myrtle M	11/1892	10/1892
SE	7	7	Branum	Katie	12/1892	12/1862
SW	11	4	Bickerstaff	Lou M	01/1893	01/1852
SW	6	7	Cameron	Mary Elizabeth RITCHEY	01/1893	08/1827

NE	6	22	Vaughn	Infant Son	03/1893	03/1893
SW	7	5	Moore	Hiram Columbus	05/1893	01/1849
SW	10	1	Ward	Thomas Jefferson	07/1893	11/1859
NE	7	25	Steen	Lola G	10/1893	05/1893
NE	8	24	Miller	Bular B	01/1894	06/1874
SW	2	5	Wiggs	Benjamin Rufus	01/1894	01/1837
SW	9	17	Berry	J	03/1895	09/1887
NE	9	27	Vaughn	James M	10/1895	12/1860
SW	10	2	Ward	Mary Frances HENSLEE	10/1895	08/1869
SE	9	10	Low/Lowe	William (II) M	04/1896	03/1818
NE	5	27	Burns	Stanley	01/1897	01/1896
SW	9	18	Berry	Merica L.	07/1898	02/1889
SW	4	1	Burns	Elmo Lee	10/1899	11/1878
SE	2	16	Wilson	Collins	01/1900	01/1889
SW	6	6	Cameron	Missouri	02/1900	03/1855

				Ann Sue BURNS		
SE	1	27	Garrett	Arwildy Jane CLARK	04/1900	09/1873
NE	8	23	Miller	Samuel Eli	06/1901	01/1841

Bibliography

A.S. Broadfoot, Mrs. 1967. "History Highlights of the Mt Zion Churches and Cemetery." Hopkins County, Texas: self-published.

Beard, Richard. 1867. *Brief Biographical Sketches of Some of the Early Ministers of the Cumberland Presybterian Church.* Nashville, Tennessee: D.D. Southern Methodist Publishing House.

Brackenridge, R. Douglas. 1968. *Voice in the Wilderness: A History of the Cumberland Presbyterian Church in Texas.* San Antonio: Trinity University Press.

c, Maredia Haddock. n.d.

Campbell, Randolph B. 2003. *Gone to Texas.* New York: Oxford University Press.

Campbell, Thomas H. 2017. *History of the Cumberland Presbyterian Church in Texas.* Memphis, Tennessee: The Cumberland Presbyterian Church.

Contributed by June England Tuck, dated DEC 1942, ed. 1924. *Daily News-Telegram*, Dec.

Cordry, Eugene Allen. 1976. *History of New Lebanon Cooper County Missouri.*

Covington, Carolyn Callaway. 2010. *Runaway Scrape.* Accessed 2018. https://tshaonline.org/handbook/online/articles/pfr01.

Cunningham, Maredia Haddock. 2016. "explanation for the concrete tomb in Mt Zion." Ancestry.com.

Elazar, Daniel Judah. 2004. *Opening Cybernetic Frontiers: Cities of the Prairie.* New Jersey, New Jersey: Transaction Publishers. Accessed 2018.

Fullmore, Z.T. c1915. *The history and geography of Texas: as told in county names.* Austin, Texas: E.L. Steck.

Good, Marty. 2016. *What is a scatter garden.* October 21. Accessed April 3, 2018. https://www.burialplanning.com/blog/2016/oct/21/what-is-a-scatter-garden/.

Haddock, Billy D. TBA. *Pillars of Mt. Zion: History of Western Hopkins County and the Branom Community.* College Station, Texas: Pending publication.

—. 2011. *Wounded Healer.* College Station, Texas: Silent Partners.

Harlin, Cyndi. 2016. "http://hcgstx.org/wp-content/uploads/2017/03/Hopkins-County-Texas-Cyndi-Harlin.pdf." *http://hcgstx.org.* Accessed September 5, 2017. http://hcgstx.org/wp-content/uploads/2017/03/Hopkins-County-Texas-Cyndi-Harlin.pdf.

2015. *https://www.fumccommerce.org.* Accessed february 2018. https://www.fumccommerce.org/about-2/history/.

Kellemen, Dr. Bob. 2014. *http://www.rpmministries.org/2014/01/are-you-a-church-pioneer-or-a-church-settler/.* January 18. Accessed September 16, 2017. http://www.rpmministries.org.

Kepner, Lisa. 2010. *https://tshaonline.org/handbook/online/articles/fyazp.*

June 15. Accessed March 3, 2018.

Linder, Joseph L. Clark and Dorothy A. 1963. *The Story of Texas.*
Boston: D. C. Heath and Company.

Lytle, Clarence Jesse, interview by Dr. James Conrad. 1985. *Roads
in Texas During the 30's and 40's* Oral History Program,
Special Collections, TAMUC Libraries, (June 19).

McCuistion, Ed H. 1995. *Loose Leaves of the History of Lamar
County.* Edited by Compiler Betsy Mills. Paris, Texas: North
Texas Publishing Company.

McDonald, J. C. 1928.
http://files.usgwarchives.net/tx/hopkins/history. Edited by
Submitted by June E. Tuck. Accessed Feburary 17, 2018.
http://files.usgwarchives.net/tx/hopkins/history/mcdonal
d1.txt.

McFarland, Carl L. 2010.
https://tshaonline.org/handbook/online/articles/kbc14.
Texas State Historical Association. June 12. Accessed
March 27, 2018.
https://tshaonline.org/handbook/online/articles/kbc14.

Moore, Stephen L. 2007. *Savage Frontier.* Vol. III. Denton, Texas:
University of North Texas. Accessed 9 16, 2017.

—. n.d. *Savage Frontier, Volume III.*

Museum, Star of the Republic. 2017.
www.txindependence.org/pdfs/texas_timeline.pdf. Blinn
College. September 5. Accessed September 9/5/2017,
2017. www.txindependence.org/pdfs/texas_timeline.pdf.

Nolan, William Kenneth (Bill). 2011.
"http://www.rosstexascavalrybrigade.com/9thtexascavalr
yregiment/index9.html."
http://www.rosstexascavalrybrigade.com. Accessed s
2017.

Otis Chandler. 2018.
*https://www.goodreads.com/author/quotes/15647074.M
ary_Reynolds.* Accessed April 3, 2018.
https://www.goodreads.com/author/quotes/15647074.M
ary_Reynolds.

n.d. *palo-duro-canyon.* Accessed Feburary 24, 2018.
https://tpwd.texas.gov/state-parks/palo-duro-canyon.

Pressler, Charles W. & Lungkwitz, Herman. 1872. "Map of Hopkins
County, map, 1872." University of North Texas Libraries,
The Portal to Texas History. Accessed September 9, 2017.
texashistory.unt.edu.

1988–1989., — adapted from an article written for the Texas
Almanac, ed. 2018. *RELIGION IN EARLY TEXAS.*
https://texasalmanac.com/topics/history/religion-early-
texas.

Richardson, T.C. c1940. *East Texas: Its history and its makers. Vol.
III.* New York: Lewis Historical Publishing Co.

Rollins, Yvonne Stewart, ed. 2002. *Mt. Zion: its history, its
churches, its schools, its families, and its folks.* Second
printing. Commerce, Texas: Texas A&M University-
Commerce Print Shop.

Rusch, Elizabeth. 2011. *Smithsonian Magazine.* December.

Accessed January 2018.
https://www.smithsonianmag.com/science-nature/the-great-midwest-earthquake-of-1811-46342/.

S. Karger AG, Basel. 2008. *https://www.ncbi.nlm.nih.gov.*
Accessed 2 21, 2018.
https://www.ncbi.nlm.nih.gov/pubmed/18264009.

Strauss, Neil Howe and William. 1992. *Generations: The History of America's Future.* New York: Harper-Collins.

Sturdivant, D.A. 1935. "The Early Days in Hopkins County." Edited by D.A. Sturdivant. from the files of Jane E. Tuck. Accessed 12 15, 2017.
http://www.rootsweb.ancestry.com/~txhopkin/gen/resources/histories/community/early_days.html.

Taylor, Carol Coley. 2005.
"http://www.carolctaylor.com/Violence%20and%20Deception.pdf." *http://www.carolctaylor.com.* Accessed September 5, 2017.
http://www.carolctaylor.com/Violence%20and%20Deception.pdf.

Tuck, June E. undated. *Cumby Rustler, 1908.* Edited by Editor and Prop. G. M. Morton. Accessed October 9, 2017.
http://files.usgwarchives.net/tx/hopkins/history/cumby1908.txt.

Tuck, Mrs. Jane. 1932. "The History of Black Jack Grove." *Hopkins County Historical Society.* Edited by assisted by the Daughters of Black Jack Grove. Hopkins County, Sulphur Springs, Texas, July 17. Accessed September 6, 2017.

unknown. undated. *Roadside Thoughts: A Gazetteer for the United States and Canada.* Accessed 10 11, 2017. https://roadsidethoughts.com/tx/branom-xx-hopkins-genealogy.htm.

Wilson, Joseph M. 1859. *Presbyterian Historical Alamanac.* Vol. One. Philidelphia.

2012. *www.accessgenealogy.com.* Accessed 2018. https://www.accessgenealogy.com/dataset/hopkins-county-texas.

ABOUT THE AUTHOR

Billy D. Haddock, born in the Branom Community, has worked at Texas A&M-Commerce as a graduate student and administrator early in his career and, later, as a psychotherapist, business consultant, and writer. He is retired from counseling in the public and private sectors with over 30 years' experience. He holds a Ph.D. in Educational Psychology from Texas A&M University and currently lives in College Station, Texas.

www.ingramcontent.com/pod-product-compliance
Lightning Source LLC
Chambersburg PA
CBHW081138090426
42736CB00018B/3398